BLACK SABBATH
& PHILOSOPHY

The Blackwell Philosophy and Pop Culture Series
Series Editor: William Irwin

24 and Philosophy
*Edited by Jennifer Hart Weed,
Richard Davis, and Ronald Weed*

30 Rock and Philosophy
Edited by J. Jeremy Wisnewski

Alice in Wonderland and
Philosophy
Edited by Richard Brian Davis

Arrested Development and
Philosophy
*Edited by Kristopher Phillips and
J. Jeremy Wisnewski*

The Avengers and Philosophy
Edited by Mark D. White

Batman and Philosophy
*Edited by Mark D. White and
Robert Arp*

Battlestar Galactica and Philosophy
Edited by Jason T. Eberl

The Big Bang Theory and
Philosophy
Edited by Dean Kowalski

The Big Lebowski and Philosophy
Edited by Peter S. Fosl

The Daily Show and Philosophy
Edited by Jason Holt

Family Guy and Philosophy
Edited by J. Jeremy Wisnewski

Final Fantasy and Philosophy
*Edited by Jason P. Blahuta and
Michel S. Beaulieu*

Game of Thrones and Philosophy
Edited by Henry Jacoby

The Girl with the Dragon Tattoo
and Philosophy
Edited by Eric Bronson

Green Lantern and Philosophy
*Edited by Jane Dryden and
Mark D. White*

Heroes and Philosophy
Edited by David Kyle Johnson

House and Philosophy
Edited by Henry Jacoby

The Hunger Games and Philosophy
*Edited by George Dunn and
Nicolas Michaud*

Inception and Philosophy
Edited by David Johnson

Iron Man and Philosophy
Edited by Mark D. White

Mad Men and Philosophy
*Edited by James South and
Rod Carveth*

Metallica and Philosophy
Edited by William Irwin

The Office and Philosophy
Edited by J. Jeremy Wisnewski

South Park and Philosophy
Edited by Robert Arp

Spider-Man and Philosophy
Edited by Jonathan Sanford

Terminator and Philosophy
*Edited by Richard Brown and
Kevin Decker*

True Blood and Philosophy
*Edited by George Dunn and
Rebecca Housel*

Twilight and Philosophy
*Edited by Rebecca Housel and
J. Jeremy Wisnewski*

The Ultimate Harry Potter and
Philosophy
Edited by Gregory Bassham

The Ultimate Lost and Philosophy
Edited by Sharon Kaye

Watchmen and Philosophy
Edited by Mark D. White

X-Men and Philosophy
*Edited by Rebecca Housel and
J. Jeremy Wisnewski*

BLACK SABBATH & PHILOSOPHY

MASTERING REALITY

Edited by William Irwin

WILEY-BLACKWELL

A John Wiley & Sons, Ltd., Publication

This edition first published 2013
© 2013 John Wiley & Sons, Inc.

Wiley-Blackwell is an imprint of John Wiley & Sons, formed by the merger of Wiley's
global Scientific, Technical and Medical business with Blackwell Publishing.

Registered Office
John Wiley & Sons, Ltd, The Atrium, Southern Gate, Chichester, West Sussex, PO19 8SQ, UK

Editorial Offices
350 Main Street, Malden, MA 02148-5020, USA
9600 Garsington Road, Oxford, OX4 2DQ, UK
The Atrium, Southern Gate, Chichester, West Sussex, PO19 8SQ, UK

For details of our global editorial offices, for customer services, and for information about how
to apply for permission to reuse the copyright material in this book please see our website at
www.wiley.com/wiley-blackwell.

The right of William Irwin to be identified as the author of the editorial material in this work
has been asserted in accordance with the UK Copyright, Designs and Patents Act 1988.

Wiley also publishes its books in a variety of electronic formats. Some content that appears in
print may not be available in electronic books.

Designations used by companies to distinguish their products are often claimed as trademarks.
All brand names and product names used in this book are trade names, service marks,
trademarks or registered trademarks of their respective owners. The publisher is not associated
with any product or vendor mentioned in this book. This publication is designed to provide
accurate and authoritative information in regard to the subject matter covered. It is
sold on the understanding that the publisher is not engaged in rendering professional services.
If professional advice or other expert assistance is required, the services of a competent
professional should be sought.

Library of Congress Cataloging-in-Publication Data
Black Sabbath and philosophy : mastering reality / edited by William Irwin.
     p.   cm. – (The Blackwell philosophy and pop culture series)
   Includes bibliographical references and index.
     ISBN 978-1-118-39759-6 (pbk.) – ISBN 978-1-118-39760-2 (emobi) –
ISBN 978-1-118-39761-9 (epub)   1. Black Sabbath (Musical group)   2. Music and
philosophy.   3. Rock music–History and criticism.   I. Irwin, William, 1970–
   ML421.B57B54 2012
   782.42166092′2–dc23
                                                   2012026658
A catalogue record for this book is available from the British Library.

Cover photograph: © Michael Ochs Archives/Getty Images
Cover design: Wendy Mount

Set in 10.5/13pt Sabon by SPi Publisher Services, Pondicherry, India
Printed by Courier/Westford

1   2013

Dedicated to Connie Santisteban, the muse of pop culture who has guided this book series

Contents

Introduction
"What Is This That Stands Before Me?"

The tape would stop in the middle of "N.I.B." whenever Ozzy sang "My name is Lucifer, please take my hand." That was enough to convince my 13-year-old self that something sinister was at work. The play button would pop up, and I would freak out. Together the songs produced a witches' brew of guilt, fear, fascination, and intoxication. Listening to Sabbath I felt that I was doing something forbidden yet necessary, like losing my virginity. Maybe I should have heeded the tape's ominous warning, but here I am 30 years later. Adolescent obsession has become adult appreciation.

We don't just listen to Black Sabbath; we are haunted by them. The music and lyrics stay with us long after the songs stop playing. There is genius in the simplicity of the unforgettable riffs, and there is hidden depth in the lyrics, which confront existential despair, social instability, political corruption, the horrors of war, and the nature of evil. The name of the band is Black Sabbath, but don't be misled. They are all about shades of gray. As with most great art, Sabbath's songs are rich, suggestive, and ambiguous, often undercutting one message with its opposite. Sabbath flirt with the occult but embrace the divine. They tell cautionary tales of heroin's hand of doom while themselves snowblind or high on sweet leaf. And they don't passively plead to give peace a chance to the tune of jangling guitars; they rage in the "*fight* for peace" to the beat of war drums. Paradoxically, their anti-war lyrics, infused with hope and love, are sung to the tune of pounding, hyper-masculine music.

Black Sabbath are the Beatles of heavy metal. They changed everything. More than 40 years later, Sabbath's music is still too aggressive for most people, and it's still not played on the oldies station. But questions linger. What makes Sabbath sound evil? Is evil in the ear of the beholder? What personal and cultural conditions led them to create heavy metal? Is it still Black Sabbath without Ozzy? Is it still Black Sabbath when Tony Iommi is the only original member? We don't aim to give the final word in answer to these questions, but we do aim to challenge the reader and stir the cauldron a bit.

Contrary to the Spinal Tap stereotype, Sabbath inspires deep thought. And this book brings together professional deep thinkers—most are philosophy professors by trade—to address some perennial questions. Philosophy is the love of wisdom; it is about discovering truth and facing reality. And, as it turns out, Plato, Aristotle, Schopenhauer, and Nietzsche can help us take Ozzy, Tony, Geezer, and Bill to a deeper level. But keep in mind that our interpretations of Sabbath's lyrics aim to highlight the philosophical significance of the lyrics rather than to recover their original intention.

Each chapter is meant to stand alone. So, although the chapters have been arranged in an order that makes sense, they can be read in any order you choose. This also means that some of the chapters overlap in the biographical information they recount and the songs they discuss. You'll read about the back streets of Birmingham and the opening lines of the song "Black Sabbath" more than once. The contributing authors don't all agree with each other, and the reader certainly isn't obliged to agree with their interpretations. This is more about questions and opinions than answers and facts.

Because of the excitement about the reunion of the original line-up announced on 11/11/11, this book focuses primarily on the Ozzy years. While that may disappoint some fans, the good news is that we have left the door open for a follow-up book, *Heaven & Hell and Philosophy*. Nor do we deal much with Ozzy's solo career. So who knows? There may be two more books to come!

We're taking Sabbath seriously and we're not apologizing. So if you'd like to master reality, start reading *Black Sabbath and Philosophy*. We'll introduce you to your mind.

Acknowledgments
They Sold Their Souls for Rock 'n' Roll

No book about Sabbath would be complete without liner notes. But you won't find here a list of famous musicians or guitar manufacturers. Nothing so exciting. You will, though, find the names of some awesome people. If you ever have the chance to meet any of these folks you'll be glad you did.

For taking me through a hole in the sky and dealing with my megalomania, I thank all my friends from the metal daze of my misspent youth, especially Sissy Dugan, Rob Guldner, J.R. Lombardo, Troy Marzziotti, and Joe Schmidt.

For providing great insight and saving me from making mistakes with this book, I thank James Bondarchuk, Per Broman, Jason Eberl, Søren R. Frimodt-Møller, Ted Gracyk, Joel McIver, and Sandy Shapshay.

For her unflagging enthusiasm and support, I thank Connie Santisteban and her team at Wiley. They have been a joy to work with on this book and on this series. I owe Connie and Co. a debt of gratitude that will not soon be repaid. For coming in to finish the job and bring this book through production and into stores, I thank Jeff Dean and his team at Wiley-Blackwell. I am very fortunate to work with such professionals.

For offering invaluable feedback on every chapter of this book, I thank Joseph Bongiorno, author of the forthcoming book, *Black Sabbath: The Illustrated Lyrics*. No one knows more about Sabbath's lyrics than Joe.

For being a great team and for teaching me lots about both Sabbath and philosophy, I thank the contributing authors of this book. It has been a pleasure to work with you and I hope I'll have the opportunity to work with you again.

I wish I could thank Ozzy, Tony, Geezer, and Bill for being personal friends of mine who helped make this book a reality. But to me they are larger-than-life figures before whom I would simply bow like Wayne and Garth, proclaiming that I'm not worthy. Still, I thank them for the music that means so much to me and without which this book would just have the rather silly title *And Philosophy*.

Most of all, I thank some people I know very well, my wife Megan from Mayberry and my two headbanging children, Daniel and Kate.

Part I
NECESSARY EVIL

Chapter 1

Beyond Good and Evil
Facing Your Demons With Black Sabbath and Existentialism

William Irwin

You know about the lost Black Sabbath album, right? They recorded it with Ozzy in 1999, but legal battles kept it from being released. It was supposed to be called *Beyond Good and Evil*. Here's the track list:

Side A

1. Fear and Trembling (instrumental) / The Plague
2. The Birth of Tragedy
3. The Devil and the Good Lord
4. Beyond Good and Evil

Side B

5. The Fall
6. Twilight of the Idols
7. The Antichrist
8. Roads to Freedom (instrumental) / No Exit

Of course, as a never-say-die Sabbath fan, you know there is no lost album. Still, this could easily be a list of Sabbath song titles. What it really is, though, is a list of book titles, books written by existentialist philosophers: Søren Kierkegaard (1813–1855), Friedrich Nietzsche

Black Sabbath and Philosophy: Mastering Reality, First Edition. Edited by William Irwin.
© 2013 John Wiley & Sons, Inc. Published 2013 by John Wiley & Sons, Inc.

(1844–1900), Jean-Paul Sartre (1905–1980), and Albert Camus (1913–1960).[1] As the titles indicate, the existentialists, like Sabbath, play with dark, macabre, and blasphemous themes.

So what is existentialism? Like heavy metal, it's notoriously difficult to define, but here's a definition anyway: Existentialism is a philosophy that reacts to an absurd or meaningless world by urging individuals to overcome alienation, oppression, and despair through freedom and self-creation. Although existentialism is most closely identified with nineteenth- and twentieth-century European philosophers, it's actually a timeless and potentially universal worldview. So we should not be surprised to see it unwittingly expressed by a British heavy metal band. In fact, I'd say Sabbath is Britain's chief contribution to existentialism.

"Life Has No Meaning, and Death's His Only Friend"

Since I discovered them at age 13, Black Sabbath have always been about facing my demons, about rebellion in response to the absurdity of life. By "the absurd" existentialists mean the lack of fit between what humans desire and how life actually is. The desire for romantic love and the inability to find or maintain it is absurd. The desire for good people to be happy and prosper and for bad people to suffer and fail is absurd. The world does not work that way. The desire for everlasting life is absurd. One day we each will cease to exist; this is a primary concern for the existentialists, leading some to conclude that life is without objective meaning.

In the novel *Nausea*, Sartre's main character, Antoine Roquentin, realizes that "Every existing thing is born without reason, prolongs itself out of weakness, and dies by chance."[2] Likewise, in "Johnny Blade," Sabbath sings: "Life has no meaning / And death's his only friend / Will fate surprise him?/Where will he meet his end? / He feels so bitter / Yes he's so full of hate / To die in the gutter / I guess that's Johnny's fate." Sabbath depicts a disenchanted world in which all angels' wings have been clipped, a world in which happiness seems impossible and life seems meaningless. What is the point of living? It's a world in which "there's never been a winner / Try your hardest, just to be a loser / The world will still be turning when you're gone" ("Wheels of Confusion").

Warbling, nasal, and uncertain, the voice of early Sabbath is tortured, haunted, alienated, and angry. The voice is not elegant, commanding, or masterful. Ozzy Osbourne is not Robert Plant, or Rob Halford, or Ronnie James Dio, or Bruce Dickinson. But to the budding existentialist, Ozzy is something better. Despite being utterly unique, Ozzy's voice has an everyman quality that made millions feel that someone else felt the way they did. Despite hitting high notes, he nonetheless sounded masculine and angry. Despite fame and adulation, Ozzy remained alienated and ill at ease. Despite being biologically old enough to be my father, he spoke to my adolescent angst, fueling my middle-class rebellion. And despite Geezer Butler writing most of the lyrics, Ozzy made them his own—they don't sound right with anyone else singing.

People think the narrator of "Paranoid" is "insane" because he's "frowning all the time." But it's pretty hard not to frown in a world like ours, and people who are put off by a frown may be wearing false smiles to delude themselves. "Paranoid" expresses angst, despair, and hopelessness: "All day long I think of things/But nothing seems to satisfy / Think I'll lose my mind / If I don't find something to pacify." What makes life worthwhile is elusive: "I need someone to show me / The things in life that I can't find / I can't see the things that make true happiness / I must be blind/Make a joke and I will sigh / And you will laugh and I will cry / Happiness I cannot feel / And love to me is so unreal." Indeed, Camus says that the only truly serious philosophical problem is determining whether life is worth living. (By the way, the name is pronounced Cam-oo.) The song's narrator seems to have concluded that life is not worth living, at least for him, though he expresses hope that the listener will nonetheless be able to find meaning and happiness: "And so as you hear these words / Telling you now of my state / I tell you to enjoy life / I wish I could but it's too late." And "Paranoid" is not just an isolated moment of melancholy. Rather, the mood pervades Sabbath's catalog. As another example, consider "Lord of this World," in which the narrator describes being stuck in an existential morass: "You're searching for your mind don't know where to start / can't find the key to fit the lock on your heart / you think you know but you are never quite sure / your soul is ill but you will not find a cure."

The narrator of "Paranoid" looks to other people to show him the way to love and happiness, but, as Sartre tells us in No Exit, "Hell is other people."[3] The narrator of "Paranoid" is thought crazy because of his constant frown. People don't see inside us; they only see the surface, the smile or frown. And so they tend to alienate us, label us, oppress us, stigmatize us, and treat us like things. Consider the plight of Iron Man, who has saved the world, and yet, in his catatonic state, is looked at as a mindless thing rather than a suffering person: "Is he alive or dead? / Has he thoughts within his head? / We'll just pass him there / Why should we even care?" Predictably, Iron Man reacts with anger to the uncaring, dehumanizing stare of other people: "Planning his vengeance / That he will soon unfurl."

For me, nothing has brought about as much existential despair as failure with women, the failure to win love and the failure to maintain love. So it's not surprising to find Sabbath's lyrics juxtaposing existential despair and the loss of love in "Solitude." At first, the song simply seems to be about overwhelming sadness: "My name it means nothing / My fortune is less / My future is shrouded in dark wilderness / Sunshine is far away, clouds linger on." Then we get the clue that the sadness is triggered by loss: "Everything I possessed—now they are gone." But in the end it becomes clear that "Solitude" is specifically about the loss of love: "The world is a lonely place—you're on your own / Guess I will go home—sit down and moan. / Crying and thinking is all that I do / Memories I have remind me of you." As Sabbath and the existentialists remind us, other people cannot generally be counted on to bring us happiness; they are more likely to make us miserable.

"I've Seen the Future and I've Left It Behind"

While Sabbath's doomy riffs form the soundtrack for existentialist despair, the driving drums and guitar leads represent freedom and rebellion. Music is emotional and, unlike most traditional philosophy, existentialism recognizes the validity of emotions. Love, anger, jealousy, pity, and pride are not to be bridled by reason but given free rein to help us make sense of the world.

With its emotional rebellion, Sabbath, like existentialism, stands for an ethics of personal responsibility. Though they may bemoan the harsh nature of reality, they don't count on anyone else to take care of them. They don't make excuses; they accept reality and embrace freedom.

The Sabs are not whiney political rock stars, blaming government or society for their problems. Rather, as unwitting existentialists, they see the fundamentally absurd nature of life as calling for a response that demands that each individual make free choices and take responsibility for the person he is and will become.

Existentialism is not a philosophy of wallowing, but a call for overcoming. Consider "Tomorrow's Dream," in which Sabbath offers a depiction of existential despair and a need for escape to a better reality: "Yes I'm leaving the sorrow and heartache / Before it takes me away from my mind / . . . / When sadness fills my days / It's time to turn away / And let tomorrow's dreams / Become reality to me."

To transcend a desperate situation, one must first face it. In this way, Nietzsche's outrageous claim that "God is dead" is echoed in the blasphemy of Sabbath's celebration of Satan in songs such as "N.I.B." It is perfectly understandable why people take flight from reality and find comfort in religion, but Nietzsche finds Christianity to be a dangerous fiction that discourages people from living this life to the fullest. (By the way, "Nietzsche" rhymes with "pleased-ta-meetchya.") As he says, "all things have been baptized in the well of eternity and are beyond good and evil; and good and evil themselves are but intervening shadows and damp depressions and drifting clouds."[4] In "Supernaut" we can hear existentialism's rejection of religion and its ethic of rugged individualism and self-reliance: "Got no religion / Don't need no friends / Got all I want / And I don't need to pretend / Don't try to reach me / 'cause I'll tear up your mind / I've seen the future / And I've left it behind."

More emotional than intellectual, Sabbath's existentialism has a rebel-without-a-cause mentality. Think of Brando in *The Wild One* when he replies to the question "What are you rebelling against?" with "Whaddya got?" Rebellion often at first involves destruction without creation to replace what is destroyed. So while despair is acknowledged, it is not yet overcome. When the comforts of religion are rejected, drugs and alcohol can become the real opium of the people. And so it isn't surprising to find Sabbath celebrating an escape to alternate reality in "Snowblind" and "Fairies Wear Boots." No song, though, captures the love and promise in the refuge of getting high better than "Sweet Leaf": "My life was empty forever on a down / Until you took me, showed me around / My life is free now, my life is clear / I love you sweet leaf—though you can't hear."

Sabbath's battles with substance abuse are well-known. Clearly, the answer to overcoming existential despair could not be found in a bottle, pipe, line, needle, or pill. To a great extent, though, the answer could be found in making music. As Nietzsche says, "what is good and evil no one knows yet, unless it be he who creates. He, however, creates man's goal and gives the earth its meaning and its future. That anything at all is good and evil—that is his creation."[5] In line with this Nietzschean insight, a note of tempered optimism from "Children of the Grave" tells us that a better world can be made: "So you children of the world, listen to what I say / If you want a better place to live in spread the word today / Show the world that love is still alive you must be brave / Or you children of today are children of the grave." As Sabbath's sonic output testifies, Nietzsche is right: Creativity, especially artistic creativity, is the proper response to pain and difficulty in life.[6]

"I Just Believe in Myself, 'Cause No One Else Is True"

While creating music is a great way to respond to life's trials and tribulations, existentialism is ultimately about creating your self. As Sartre says, "Man is nothing but that which he makes of himself,"[7] and we are "condemned to be free."[8] This means we are free to make ourselves or free to abdicate choice and become what society makes of us. Someone who is free of self-deception and truly faces up to his choices and their consequences is authentic, a genuine person. The authentic individual is not obliged to make one decision rather than another, for example to join the army or protest the war, but he is required to fully realize that the choice he has made was a free one and is his own responsibility.

The existentialist opposes conformity for the sake of conformity. By going along with the crowd in their choice of values, one loses sight of oneself as a free individual. Though existential despair is not a good thing, many people avoid it only by not being genuine individuals. Instead they simply live, act, choose, and decide in the way the rest of the crowd does. These are the kind of people "Never Say Die" expresses disapproval of, people who are led by societal norms, "People going nowhere / Taken for a ride." Likewise, "Under the Sun/ Every Day Comes and Goes," a title that alludes to the book of

Ecclesiastes, also presents an image of people around us living inauthentic lives in "bad faith," a kind of self-deception and denial of the freedom to choose one's individual identity: "People hiding their real face / Keep on running their rat race / Behind each flower grows a weed / In their world of make-believe."

Of course, there is a temptation to feel superior to the masses of people who live like anonymous members of the herd, but ultimately the focus must be on oneself, leaving others to lead their superficial lives. "Cornucopia" nicely captures the way people live in bad faith, deceiving themselves: "Too much near the truth they say / Keep it 'til another day / Let them have their little game / Delusion helps to keep them sane / Let them have their little toys / Matchbox cars and mortgaged joys / Exciting in their plastic ways / Frozen food in a concrete maze." After all, there is a price to be paid by those who will face reality and make meaningful works of art of their very lives. An artist must suffer for his art, and this is no less true of the person who sculpts himself into an authentic individual. "Cornucopia" captures this creative struggle with the lines, "I don't know what's happening / My head's all torn inside / People say I'm heavy / They don't know what I hide." And the narrator of "Under the Sun/Every Day Comes and Goes," leaves us with this existential advice: "Just believe in yourself—you know you really shouldn't have to pretend / Don't let those empty people try to interfere with your mind / Just live your life and leave them all behind."

In a world that defies our desires, a world populated by plastic people, it's easy to fall prey to righteous indignation. We're told that Johnny Blade is "a victim of modern frustration / That's the reason he's so ready to fight." We're also told "He's the one that should be afraid," when the narrator wonders, "What will happen to you, Johnny Blade?" As Camus sees it, we want to make sense of a world that does not make sense. It's the same impulse that has us looking for shapes and figures in the clouds. There are no shapes or figures there objectively speaking, but if we look hard enough we may think we see them. Through habits and illusions we can come to see things in the world that are not objectively there, but if those habits and illusions are stripped away, then our world will come undone. The point is to overcome the sense that life on this planet is hostile and absurd and instead to just accept "the gentle indifference of the world," as Camus calls it. One must come to realize that the universe itself is not absurd; only our relationship with it is absurd. The world is not unfair or irrational; it's just that our demands make it seem that way.

The mythological character Sisyphus is emblematic of "modern frustration." He is condemned by the gods to roll a rock to the top of a hill every day only to have the rock roll back down again. In retelling the myth, Camus famously says, "The struggle itself toward the heights is enough to fill a man's heart. One must imagine Sisyphus happy."[9] This means we don't need a higher purpose. We're not even as lucky as Sisyphus to have the gods so interested in our lives as to punish us. Our very existence is without pre-given meaning, yet that's OK. We don't need a pre-given purpose, and we can deal with a universe that is indifferent to us, a world that allows our rocks to roll down hills. The struggle to live in the face of all of this is enough to fill our hearts and make us happy. We are free to choose how we will live our lives; nothing necessarily compels us to do one thing or another. In making our free choices we define who we are. Along these lines, "Under the Sun/Every Day Comes and Goes" presents an existentialist's declaration of independence: "Well I don't want no preacher / Telling me about the god in the sky / No I don't want no one to tell me / Where I'm gonna go when I die / I wanna live my life with no people telling me what to do / I just believe in myself, 'cause no one else is true."

Unfinished Symphonies

As we know from the history of Black Sabbath, progress in overcoming alienation, oppression, and despair through freedom and self-creation is not always straightforward. There are existential slips back into the comforts of drugs, religion, and bad faith. We don't often get Hollywood happy endings in Black Sabbath songs or existentialist novels, but we do get hope. And we do get the symptom of the universe, a love that never dies. Even though other people often oppress us, stigmatize us, and disappoint us, we can't live without them. We need to love both romantically and otherwise in order to have hope.

As self-made works of art, the Sabs are works in progress, unfinished symphonies. In facing their demons, they help us face our own. What more could we ask?[10]

Notes

1. Other Sabbathesque titles by existentialists include: *Dirty Hands*, *The Rebel*, *The Stranger*, *The Fall*, *The Just Assassins*, *Reflections on the Guillotine*, *A Happy Death*, *The Sickness unto Death*, *The Concept of Dread*, *A Very Easy Death*, and *Who Shall Die?*
2. Jean-Paul Sartre, *Nausea* (New York: New Directions Publishing, 1964), 133.
3. Jean-Paul Sartre, *No Exit and Three Other Plays* (New York: Vintage International, 1989), 45. Strictly speaking, it is the character Garcin who says this, but the view fits pretty well with Sartre's view of interpersonal relationships.
4. Friedrich Nietzsche, *Thus Spoke Zarathustra* (New York: Penguin, 1966), 165–166.
5. Ibid., 196.
6. See Friedrich Nietzsche, *The Birth of Tragedy* (New York: Vintage, 1967). See also Chapter 10 in this book by Dennis Knepp, "Gods, Drugs, and Ghosts: Finding Dionysus and Apollo in Black Sabbath and the Birth of Heavy Metal."
7. Jean-Paul Sartre, "Existentialism is a Humanism," in Walter Kaufmann, ed., *Existentialism from Dostoevsky to Sartre* (New York: Meridian, 1956), 291.
8. Ibid., 295.
9. Albert Camus, *The Myth of Sisyphus and Other Essays* (New York: Vintage International, 1991), 123.
10. Many thanks to the following folks for helpful feedback on this chapter: James Bondarchuk, Joseph Bongiorno, Joanna Corwin, Jason Eberl, Søren R. Frimodt-Møller, Kyle Johnson, Dennis Knepp, Greg Littman, Megan Lloyd, J.R. Lombardo, Eileen Sweeney, and Mark White.

Chapter 2

Masters of a Better Possible Reality
Conquering Evil With Love

Liz Stillwaggon Swan

Black Sabbath's songs depict evil in the form of nuclear war ("Electric Funeral"), drug abuse ("Hand of Doom"), oppression ("Black Sabbath"), poverty ("Wicked World"), pollution ("Into the Void"), and emotional pain ("Solitude"). Ever since high school, I've been aware that Sabbath is infatuated with evil and is skilled at conjuring mental images of how bad things can get on earth. So after a couple of decades of listening to Black Sabbath, I was surprised to discover that the person behind most of the band's evil-themed lyrics, bassist Geezer Butler, is a confirmed vegan and a self-proclaimed pacifist. But then again, maybe I should've expected that. After all, the band's lyrics reveal a deep curiosity about why human nature is the way it is, and a deep sensitivity to the philosophy and poetry of real life. In fact, despite the band's focus on evil, their overall message is that it's possible to imagine and thus act to create a better possible reality.

Evil Is a Problem

Humans are often downright cruel to each other, to other animals, and even to the natural world itself. How could an all-loving, all-powerful God allow such evil? This question captures the essence of what philosophers call *the problem of evil*, which challenges believers, in the

Black Sabbath and Philosophy: Mastering Reality, First Edition. Edited by William Irwin.
© 2013 John Wiley & Sons, Inc. Published 2013 by John Wiley & Sons, Inc.

words of Bertrand Russell (1872–1970), to accept that God either exists and is evil or is "the creation of our own conscience."[1] All good philosophers define their terms, so let's begin by defining "evil." We all know what evil is—something bad. But evil differs from just plain bad in at least one crucial way: while bad can describe anything not to our liking, from a failing grade on an exam to an annoying headache to an awful movie, evil carries with it a degree of moral weight not usually attached to mere badness. When we talk about evil people or evil actions, we are making a moral judgment of the person or the action in a way that suggests that a morally preferable alternative is available.

Philosophers commonly distinguish between natural evil and moral evil. Natural evil includes everything from natural disasters—hurricanes and tsunamis that leave thousands of people dead or destitute—to disease in animals and humans, suffering caused by genetic defects, animals in the wild hunting and killing other animals, and so on. So, natural evil is comprised of unfortunate events or circumstances for which no human being is directly responsible. Moral evil, by contrast, is comprised of acts and their consequences for which human beings are directly responsible, such as war, murder, pollution, and so on. And it's this latter type of evil that is the focus of much of Sabbath's lyrics.

Ravi Zacharias, an evangelical Christian thinker, argues that although the problem of evil is intended to pose a challenge to the existence of God, in fact it unintentionally affirms the existence of God. Zacharias explains that if you posit the existence of evil, you implicitly posit the existence of good as well. And if you posit the existence of good and evil, you are implicitly positing a moral law, which entails a moral lawgiver—or in other words, God. So even to ask why there is evil in the world is to acknowledge that God exists.[2]

One could argue, however, that Zacharias simplifies things too much. Why couldn't it be possible for there to be a God who was not all-good and all-powerful but was just mostly good and mostly powerful? And why couldn't there be a moral law without there being a God?

Pictures of Evil

Before grappling with the problem of evil, let's survey some of the evil scenes in Sabbath's songs. "Electric Funeral" describes a terrifying and potentially realistic future world ravaged by nuclear war.

The storyteller describes a, "dying world of radiation" with "victims of man's frustration" and likens the world to a "burning globe of obscene fire" that looks like an "electric funeral pyre." The scene painted in the listener's mind is truly horrifying, with "Buildings crashing down / To Earth's cracking ground," while "Rivers turn to mud / Eyes melt into blood."[3] The evil of nuclear war is made frighteningly real with this song.

The dark and depressing aspects of drug addiction are the central themes in "Hand of Doom." The storyteller describes the fate of a heroin junkie spiraling out of control: "Your skin starts turning green" and "Your eyes no longer see / Life's reality." The song disturbs and upsets us, especially since nearly everyone knows an alcoholic or drug addict who has lost touch with reality, neglecting their loved ones, themselves, and their responsibilities in life. The heroin addict in this story faces "death's sickly grin," leaving holes in his skin that are caused by a "deadly pin." Imagining the demise of the addict described in the next few lines is enough to nauseate the listener, as the addict's head "starts spinning 'round" and he falls "down to the ground," feeling his body heave as "death hand starts to weave." Sadly, we know the end is near for this pitiful addict who has lost all sense of self and direction.

One of the most eerily beautiful songs in Black Sabbath's vast collection is "Solitude," which depicts existential despair and loneliness. The narrator has apparently had his heart broken unjustly and asks rhetorically, "Oh where can I go to and what can I do? / Nothing can please me only thoughts are of you," and then, speaking to his ex-lover, laments, "You just laughed when I begged you to stay / I've not stopped crying since you went away." The song sadly concludes with the observation that "the world is a lonely place—you're on your own," a situation that leaves the narrator no choice but to go home and "sit down and moan," adding that "crying and thinking is all that I do." Whoever this broken person is, our heart goes out to him because his pain from having suffered this very common human-inflicted evil—a broken heart—is something all of us can relate to.

The song "Black Sabbath" seems like the stuff of horror movies, but it can be interpreted as an allegory of social oppression. The frightened narrator begins by asking, "What is this that stands before me? / Figure in black which points at me." He turns around quickly and starts to run, only to find out that he is "the chosen one." The situation deteriorates from there with the narrator discovering that the master of ceremonies is none other than Satan himself, who sits there smiling with "eyes of fire," at which point the narrator cries out in vain for God to help him. If we interpret the song as an allegory, the accusing, mocking Satan could represent any faction of society that has the power and the will to terrorize and ultimately destroy individuals or groups of individuals it does not like, either by killing (for example, in war) or by more subtle forms of social oppression.

Clearly Black Sabbath is in touch with the darker side of humanity. But to believe that this darker side is really driven by evil could imply two questionable conclusions. First, according to Zacharias's line of thinking, to assume the existence of evil is to assume the existence of God. Second, and more importantly, to see bad things in the world as being truly evil colors them in a supernatural way that could render them essentially beyond human control, leaving us powerless against them. But this is not the way Sabbath sees evil. Their lyrics offer hope against the evil in the world, inspiring us to believe in a better possible reality by forcing us to imagine one.

One very influential view of good and evil comes from the ancient religion of Manichaeism—a widespread rival to early Christianity. Manichaeism taught that good and evil were opposing supernatural forces acting within people, causing them to do good and bad things. In fact, Sabbath's stories about warring forces of good and evil might lead you to think they have a Manichean worldview. But that would not be quite correct. Sabbath comes closer to St Augustine (354–430), who embraced Manichaeism for a time but ultimately rejected it. Augustine saw that the idea of an external force of evil allowed him to excuse himself when he did wrong and "blame this unknown thing which was in me but was not part of me."[4] Realizing that this couldn't be correct, Augustine came to conceive of evil as simply a lack of goodness, not a force in its own right. Evil human actions don't result from some supernatural evil force, but instead result from human free will when it does not choose what is good.[5] Sabbath's lyrics feature Satan and evil figures, but I would argue that Sabbath is closer to Augustine than to Manichaeism. Sabbath rejects the notion that evil is a supernatural dark force beyond our control. And although they do not solve the problem of evil, especially if we consider natural evil like tsunamis and cancer, they do have a response to evil. With their stories put to music, Sabbath depicts, and inspires us to create, a better possible reality.

Imagining a Better Reality

Black Sabbath recognizes that evil is pervasive in the world, but they do not usually look to God, whether or not he exists, to save us.[6] Instead, our salvation lies in the powerful human ability to imagine a better possible reality. Though Sabbath likes to expose the dark and ugly underbelly of humanity, they also remind us that human nature has a freer, lighter, and happier dimension that can be tapped into and made manifest in times of darkness.

"Children of the Grave" depicts a world full of evil in which we must wonder: "Will the sunrise of tomorrow bring in peace in any way? / Must the world live in the shadow of atomic fear / Can they win the fight for peace or will they disappear?" People are "tired of being pushed around / And told just what to do" and so "Revolution in their minds / The children start to march / Against the world in which they have to live / And all the hate that's in their hearts." The song's narrator could easily have wallowed in anger and despair. Or he could've called for violent rebellion. But instead he issues the instruction to fight evil with love: "If you want a better place to live in spread the word today / Show the world that love is still alive you must be brave." Sabbath is rarely pure in its optimism, though, and so the song concludes with the ominous warning that either love will prevail "Or you children of today are children of the grave."

Sabbath's call to make a better world through love and care for one another resonates with Bertrand Russell's call to action in "A Free Man's Worship":

> United with his fellow-men by the strongest of all ties, the tie of a common doom, the free man finds that a new vision is with him always, shedding over every daily task the light of love. The life of Man is a long march through the night, surrounded by invisible forces, tortured by weariness and pain, towards a goal that few can hope to reach, and where none may tarry long. One by one, as they march, our comrades vanish from our sight, seized by the silent orders of omnipotent Death. Very brief is the time in which we can help them, in which their happiness or misery is decided. Be it ours to shed sunshine on their path, to lighten their sorrows by the balm of sympathy, to give them the pure joy of a never-tiring affection, to strengthen failing courage, to instil faith in hours of despair. Let us not weigh in grudging scales their merits and demerits, but let us think only of their need—of the sorrows,

the difficulties, perhaps the blindnesses, that make the misery of their lives; let us remember that they are fellow-sufferers in the same dark- ness, actors in the same tragedy with ourselves. And so, when their day is over, when their good and their evil have become eternal by the immortality of the past, be it ours to feel that, where they suffered, where they failed, no deed of ours was the cause; but wherever a spark of the divine fire kindled in their hearts, we were ready with encourage- ment, with sympathy, with brave words in which high courage glowed.[7]

Continuing our exposition of Sabbath's message of hope, we see that "Into the Void" begins by painting a picture of a hypothetical Earth that has done itself in, where "pollution kills the air, the land and sea" and where "hateful battles rag[e] on." We are told that ambassadors of this failing Earth leave it "to all its sin and hate" and are sent out into space with the mission of finding "another world where freedom waits." This story has a happy ending, though, with the travelers finding "Love upon a land, a world unknown / Where the sons of freedom make their home" and are inspired to "leave the Earth to Satan and his slaves," leaving the people "to their future in their graves" and then "Make a home where love is there to stay / Peace and happiness in every day."

Though this story could be understood literally, it is better under- stood as an abstract, possible world, similar in nature to the biblical concept of "heaven on Earth." For Black Sabbath, evil is not so much a theological or philosophical *problem* as a very real part of life—one that challenges us to use our human ability to imagine, and try to create through our actions, a better and happier reality, with less human evil.

The "Spiral Architect" from *Sabbath Bloody Sabbath* could refer to anything from God, to the DNA molecule, to a human architect. The narrator tells the listener: "Of all the things I value most in life / I see my memories and feel their warmth / And know that they are good," explaining that "Laughter kissing love / Is showing me the way." In addition to valuing life, the narrator values the Earth itself, saying: "Of all the things I value most of all / I look upon my Earth and feel the warmth / And know that it is good." Far from evil, this heartfelt confession of love for one's world and one's life almost sounds like a prayer.

As Sabbath fans know, the "Symptom of the Universe" is "a love that never dies." In this song's beautiful love story, sunshine, happiness, and love follow years of crying oceans of tears. The narrator says, presumably to a lover, "Take my hand, my child of love, come step inside my tears / Swim the magic ocean I've been crying all these years" and explains that "with our love we'll ride away into eternal skies." He looks into the eyes of this "child of love's creation" and tells her, "I see no sadness, you are all that loving means." And he makes her a promise of unending love in saying, "Take my hand and we'll go riding through the sunshine from above / We'll find happiness together in the summer skies of love."

Evil on Stage

It is ironic that Black Sabbath has a reputation for being satanic and evil when a close analysis of their lyrics reveals that they are open to the question of God's existence, sensitive to the poetry of life, and full of compassion for the struggles of humanity. This insight into the true personality of the band has historically been overshadowed by their on-stage persona.

With bands like Black Sabbath, there is an undeniable element of on-stage badass behavior that is clearly part of the performance and not indicative of the people behind the music. As we've seen, for instance, Geezer Butler is a confirmed vegan and pacifist, clearly intent on doing no harm to either people or animals, even though his lyrics often depict the various ways we can and do hurt other people, other animals, the natural world, and ourselves. For all of Black Sabbath's images of death, destruction, pain, and suffering, there are plenty of more positive images, focusing on happiness, love, freedom, and the sunshine of summer. The members of Sabbath have proven themselves to be true poets of human nature, in touch with both the dark and the light sides of humanity, encouraging us to create, along with them, a better possible reality for humanity.

Notes

1. Bertrand Russell, "A Free Man's Worship," www.philosophicalsociety.com/Archives/A%20Free%20Man's%20Worship.htm.
2. www.rzim.org.
3. These lyrics are unclear and debated by fans. Another possibility is that Ozzy sings "rivers drained to wood, ice melting to flood."

4. Augustine, *Confessions* (Oxford: Oxford University Press, 2008), Book 5, Section 10.
5. See Augustine, *On Free Choice of the Will* (Indianapolis: Hackett, 1993).
6. "After Forever" is one notable exception.
7. Thanks to Bill Irwin for supplying me with this very fitting quotation.

Chapter 3

"Is It the End, My Friend?" Black Sabbath's Apocalypse of Horror

Brian Froese

The story is as legendary as it is serendipitous. In late 1960s Birmingham, England, a young heavy blues band named Earth settled into their new rehearsal space at the Newtown Community Centre. Convinced they needed to change their name because another band in the area also had the name Earth, they felt some urgency. Across the street was a movie theater that often played horror films, and on this particular day the cinema was playing Boris Karloff's movie *Black Sabbath*. The quartet looked on and marveled that people paid money to be frightened. Duly inspired, they named themselves Black Sabbath, down-tuned the guitar, and invoked the evil mystery of the tritone. Then on Friday the 13th, February 1970, they released their eponymous debut album, *Black Sabbath*, and heavy metal was born.

At a time when occult books by Dennis Wheatley topped bestseller lists, satanic-themed movies like *Rosemary's Baby* crushed the box office, and the Manson family murders overtook the news, a sludge-like sound thick with bass and heavy on guitar stormed both sides of the Atlantic. Soon, wearing large silver crosses to fend off a curse placed on them by an occult sect after they declined to play at Stonehenge, the lads from Birmingham brought the new reality of metal down upon youth culture.[1] Creating a lyrical cosmology that

Black Sabbath and Philosophy: Mastering Reality, First Edition. Edited by William Irwin.
© 2013 John Wiley & Sons, Inc. Published 2013 by John Wiley & Sons, Inc.

was mythic in quality, Black Sabbath recounted basic human struggles in a vast universe where forces of good and evil tear at humanity.

Birmingham Apocalypse

John "Ozzy" Osbourne, Tony Iommi, Bill Ward, and Terry "Geezer" Butler grew up in Birmingham, a blue-collar, working-class city with a bad economy and few options outside of the factories in the 1960s. They described their location—"the industrial slums of Birmingham"—succinctly as "grimy."[2] Both Iommi and Osbourne recall playing as children in the remains of buildings that had been bombed in World War II, ruined structures that also served as magnets for violent youth gangs.[3] Thus, metal was born in the apocalyptic and devilish mood of the late 1960s and early 1970s as a transgressive voice for working-class masculine disquiet. According to Iommi, Black Sabbath existed in the post-1960s hippy liberalism, posturing against the failure of "flowers in your hair" singsong bourgeois utopianism. Ozzy put it best in describing his reaction to the song "San Francisco (Be Sure to Wear Some Flowers in Your Hair)": "with everyone knackered, broke and dying from asbestos poisoning or whatever toxic shit they were breathing in every day . . . you'd hear all this hippy crap about 'gentle people' going to love-ins at Haight-Ashbury. . . . I hated those hippy-dippy songs, man."[4]

With down-tuned guitars and heavy reliance on the tritone, Black Sabbath brought a new musical sound to their audience. And they also explored a dark lyrical terrain, untouched by hippy bands. While at times their songs concerned social issues such as war and drug abuse, they more often took up dark dystopic themes and employed apocalyptic and occultist imagery.

In sum, theirs was an eschatological imagination. As members of an alienated and impoverished working class who had walked through the rubble of bombed out Birmingham on their way to school and work, Sabbath responded to the liberal 1960s middle-class counter-culture by creating sinister sounds. Their scary songs and rebellious postures were ultimately uplifting, though. As Bill Ward says, "All our songs have been about positive energy."[5] From the confluence of fright and uplift came the power of Black Sabbath.

Last Things

Iommi was raised in a nominally Catholic home; Osbourne attended Church of England Sunday School for a time; and chief lyricist Butler came from an Irish-Catholic family. So the members of Sabbath were no strangers to Christianity. In fact, according to Iommi, Butler was quite devoted to his Catholicism while maintaining an ardent interest in the fantasy fiction of J.R.R. Tolkien and the occultism of Dennis Wheatley. Ozzy even adds Aleister Crowley to this lyrical list. It was perhaps this strange blend of Christian and satanic influences that led to the band's apocalyptic and eschatological lyrics.[6]

Eschatology is the branch of Christian theology and philosophy concerned with "last things." The most famous example of Christian eschatology is the final book of the New Testament, the Book of the Revelation of Saint John the Divine (hereafter, Revelation). The imagery, metaphors, and literary devices of Revelation are numerous and well known. They include the Four Horsemen of the Apocalypse, the Beast and its mark of 666, the Antichrist, the Whore of Babylon, the Battle of Armageddon, and the Final Judgment. As a genre, apocalyptic literature in the ancient world was written for societies in collapse and communities suffering persecution. Christian eschatology, as found in Revelation, has its roots in Jewish apocalypticism especially as found in the Book of Daniel from the Hebrew Scriptures.[7]

The purpose of eschatological thought and apocalyptic writing was to exhort the suffering community to persevere. In the Christian version, although the oppressive structures of the Roman Empire were seemingly all powerful, ultimately history was in the hand of God. The promise was that, come the end of days, the faithful would live in paradise while the demonic structures of political, economic, and religious oppression would be cast away. There are many tropes in apocalyptic literature, for example, cosmic journeys in time and space, talking animals, great monsters, and otherworldly voices and visions.[8] Not surprisingly, several of these literary devices are found in the songs of Black Sabbath. The biblical scholar Elaine Pagels describes apocalyptic literature as a form of "war literature." Naturally the author of Revelation, St John of Patmos, wrote in the context of war and persecution in his own life. But the world of the 1960s and 1970s was also one of war and dystopic rumblings. The West was embroiled in the Cold War with the Soviet Union, and the threat of a nuclear holocaust loomed large. Beyond that, the United States and some of its allies were involved in a hot war against communist forces in Vietnam. In this context, even if not intentionally, Black Sabbath was writing war music and poetry with the force of apocalyptic literary style.

Ancient apocalyptic iconography and its literary influence have a "multivalent" quality. This means that although apocalyptic literature refers to specific contexts for specific audiences, people across times and cultures can read their own realities into the literature. Thus, people in different centuries and countries have seen their own world in the text of Revelation. Black Sabbath, in fact, uses the rhetorical devices of Revelation to comment upon the despair of their own world, and this is in keeping with the multivalent possibilities of apocalyptic style.[9]

Satan Smiling: War and Judgment

The first song by Black Sabbath, "Black Sabbath," on the album, *Black Sabbath* begins with the sounds of falling rain and a tolling bell before we hear the anxious protagonist: "What is this that stands before me? / Figure in black which points at me / Turn around quick, and start to run." Black Sabbath dropped the gauntlet by asking a very basic question: What am I looking at? Over the next decade they described what they saw: political hypocrisy, nuclear dread, drug-fueled licentiousness, and legal difficulties. Threaded through the catalog of their tales is an apocalyptic reading of their world. The debut song ends with an eschatological vision clearly stated: "Is it the end, my friend? / Satan's coming 'round the bend / People running 'cause they're scared." Peeling away the patina of peace and love that was the flower-power 1960s, the eponymous song "recount[s] the crisis of judgment."[10]

Satan is a recurring figure in the early Black Sabbath offerings. While in apocalyptic literature generally, Satan is not necessarily an image of endings, for Black Sabbath the evil one is often invoked for that purpose. In "Black Sabbath" he is sitting and smiling, telling the afflicted their desires. In "N.I.B." we get a sly tale of the devil. Though it seems to be a hard-rock love song, we learn eventually that this possessive missive from lover to beloved comes from the hand of Lucifer. And, alas, the beloved will not know until it is too late: only when one looks into Lucifer's eyes will all be revealed.

Of course, Black Sabbath were not the first artists to portray the power of erotic love as demonic or apocalyptic. Indeed, this portrayal has been a mainstay in art, reaching back to ancient mythology and biblical tales. "Warning" from the first album returns us to this theme, with the narrator describing the power a woman has over him as akin to such apocalyptic tropes as the sun changing shape, powerful winds, and changes in the sea. Perhaps wisely, he interprets these as a "sign" that he should have left her alone. The impact of his broken heart is global: "Now the whole wide world is movin'."

The apocalyptic use of Satan continues through some of Sabbath's war songs. In "War Pigs," an anti-Vietnam War song, we hear, "Hand of God has struck the hour / Day of Judgment, God is calling / On their knees the war pigs crawling / Begging mercy for their sins / Satan, laughing, spreads his wings." The working title of the song was "Walpurgis," which is significant, considering Geezer's interest in Crowleian occultism and considering that the twentieth chapter of Crowley's book *Moonchild* is titled "Walpurgis-Night."[11] In reality Walpurgis Night is a spring festival six months from All Hallows Eve, observed April 30–May 1. Though the festival has some roots in Christian folklore regarding an early Christian missionary to Germanic peoples, it is also the night when witches gather to welcome spring. Over time, it became a festival welcoming spring, to chase away evil spirits and ensure the fertility of land and cattle.[12] In Crowley's novel, on Walpurgis Night there is a metaphysical journey into darkness where a vision is received. In the vision worshipers at the Sabbath by Stonehenge give up their newborn babies to their respective gods, which are all assembled (and all the gods of history are present), who in turn throw the babies onto a giant web covered in insects, animals, and reptiles.[13]

Thus when a winged Satan emerges at the end of "War Pigs," laughing at all that has transpired—destruction and the dawning of God's judgment—Black Sabbath uses an ancient literary device to make real the evil nature of the monster of death. As Pagels describes this use of the monster, "while we think of dragons as creatures of folktales and children's stories, Israel's writers conjured them as images of the forces of disintegration and death that lurk in the background of our world and threaten its stability."[14] For Sabbath, the stability of the world is manifest through Satan's minions: generals and politicians as war pigs. Their judgment is coming, invoking the biblical Last Judgment, and their pathetic state is brought into relief as Satan flies away in a cackle of laughter.

For Black Sabbath, that leering dark background would be made clear again. While Vietnam brought massive destruction, napalm, and drug-addled escapism ("Hand of Doom"), a greater beast, nuclear war, was looming on the horizon. Atomic Armageddon seemed imminent, and Black Sabbath brought to the poetic battlefield searing images in which: "Plastic flowers melt in sun / Fading moon falls . . . / Rivers turn to mud / Eyes melt into blood / . . . / Supernatural king / Takes earth under his wing / Heaven's golden chorus sings / Hell's angels flap their wings / Evil souls fall to Hell / Ever trapped in burning cell" ("Electric Funeral"). With apocalyptic imagination and extreme images, Black Sabbath articulated in lyrical form a real eschatological vision of the precarious nature of their world.

Sabbath Bloody Sabbath: Death and Deliverance

Though it reveals horrors, apocalyptic literature often brings hope for deliverance. For example, Sabbath's song "Iron Man" explores the theme of saviors and destroyers: "He was turned to steel / In the great magnetic field / When he traveled time / For the future of mankind / Nobody wants him / . . . / Planning his vengeance / . . . / Kills the people he once saved." Iron Man, plotting revenge from the realm of the dead by song's end, is resurrected and "lives again." In a transvaluation of the Christian apocalyptic narrative, "Iron Man" transforms the New Testament image of the loving Savior into an anti-hero.

In Christian eschatology, the deliverance is typically deliverance from the sins and evils of the world and even from death itself. Given the Christian and Satanic influence on Black Sabbath, we shouldn't be surprised to find that in addition to the anti-hero of "Iron Man" they also give us the rebellious Christian narrator of "After Forever." Reflecting on the immortality of the soul, the resurrection of the dead, fear of death, and the reality of God, the narrator intones that such contemplation led to his conversion experience. A similar invocation is made on *Technical Ecstasy* in the song, "You Won't Change Me," with the plaintive cry: "If there's a God up there, well I hope he helps me / I need him now to set me free." In fact, this acceptance of the Christian God, made explicit with reference to those "that crucified Christ" in "After Forever," is identified as the ultimate countercultural expression: "Is your mind so small that you have to fall / In with the pack wherever they run?" The reality expressed in the song is deeply personal and is less concerned with the kind of social critique we get in "War Pigs."

Mixed in with the decaying delights of drug use and erotic longing is a fuller conception of the world Sabbath is negotiating: it is geopolitical and it is personal. Thus, while God may very well bring judgment upon those deceived by Satan, as in "War Pigs," God is also the primary actor of salvation, "The only one who can save you now from all this sin and hate." Whereas the sin and hate referenced in "After Forever" is personal, in "Children of the Grave" Black Sabbath makes the connection to larger forces of social justice and protest in the inherently apocalyptic milieu of possible atomic war.[15]

In "Lord of this World" the Christian theology of "After Forever" is reiterated. Creation of the world is ascribed to God, "someone above," our free will is affirmed, "you choose evil ways instead of love," and it is implied that the Lord of this World is Satan, the "evil possessor." Still, we should not confuse Black Sabbath's lyrical explorations with actual Christian conversion or evangelical triumph. Their depiction of the apocalyptic in the world around them is intensely personal to the point of resenting religious people in their midst: "Well I don't want no Jesus freak to tell me what it's all about / No black magician telling me to cast my soul out" ("Under the Sun/Every Day Comes and Goes").[16]

Sabbath's fifth album, Sabbath Bloody Sabbath, had cover art, titled The Rape of Christ, depicting a satanic orgy on a bed festooned with a skull, 666, and red claws.[17] It's not surprising, then, that "A National Acrobat" from Sabbath Bloody Sabbath a features a reflection on the apparent randomness of existence. In contrast with images of being chosen in "Black Sabbath" and later on "Shock Wave," "A National Acrobat" highlights the seemingly arbitrary nature of one's birth. Still, reflection on the many never born from unsuccessful sperm, does not lead to melancholy. Rather, the narrator urges us to live life to the fullest: "Treat your life for what it's worth / And live for every breath." We are told that secrets will remain secret but also that the mystery will be revealed to us at the time of our death—that we have many lives yet to live and that "love is life / And hate is living death." Yet, not all is happy in Black Sabbath's universe. Alienation and revenge form the story of the title track, "Sabbath Bloody Sabbath," where the power of isolation calls out to see "The people who have crippled you / You want to see them burn." Here "the gates of life have closed" and one hopes for "the hand of doom" to take one's mind away. Whereas Revelation and traditional eschatology is about hope for the oppressed and punishment for the oppressors, Black Sabbath locates that simple binary in a complicated present. Within a lyrical corpus that is unabashed in its contradictions—accepting and rejecting Christianity, reflecting on life through optimistic and dreadful lenses—Black Sabbath holds out for the liberation of the apocalyptic vision, through critique of society and embrace of individualism.

Planet Caravan: Journeys of Time and Space

A journey, often through time and space, is another significant literary device in apocalyptic literature. As St John "ascended . . . into the heavens," Black Sabbath employs cosmic travel.[18] Black Sabbath's first foray into cosmic travel comes via "Planet Caravan" on *Paranoid*. In a depiction of travel "through endless skies," the traveler describes the journey where celestial and terrestrial bodies are given qualities of life more typical of sentient beings: stars as eyes, a night that sighs, a moon with tears, and finally passing Mars not only as the red planet, but the god of war watching with his "crimson eye."

"Into the Void" from *Master of Reality* depicts space travel as an alternative to living in a world ruled by Satan: "Could it be the end of man and time /. . . / Leave the earth to all its sin and hate / Find another world where freedom waits /. . . / Leave the earth to Satan and his slaves / . . . / Make a home where love is there to stay." On the next album, *Vol. 4*, the song "Supernaut" also describes cosmic travel, speeding through the sky "to touch the sun." But this time the cosmic travel is radical in its individualism: "Got no religion / Don't need no friends . . . I've seen the future / And I've left it behind." Significantly, Sabbath returns to the theme of cosmic travel on *Sabotage* with the song "Hole in the Sky." This time the destination is heaven itself: "gateway to heaven / Window in time / Through it I fly / I've seen the stars that disappear in the sun / . . . / And even though I'm sitting waiting for Mars / I don't believe there's any future . . . / . . . / I've watched the dogs of war enjoying their feast / I've seen the western world go down in the east / The food of love became the greed of our time." In these cosmic travelogues, as in biblical apocalyptic, the trauma of a fading existence on earth is replaced by the hope of the larger force of love.

The End Is Near

Black Sabbath presents a sacralized universe. If Christian apocalyptic hope failed, the new post-industrial metal messiah would not. Thus, in protesting their own sense of marginality, Black Sabbath produced an imaginative cosmology. Their songs reconstruct Christian images, in particular those of the apocalypse, which, in the industrial working-class context they came from, had failed to articulate a teleological vision congruent with the contradictions of modern post-war life.

Ultimately, the first incarnation of Black Sabbath came full circle. On the eve of Ozzy's firing from the band, the ironically titled album *Never Say Die!* was released. Their first song, "Black Sabbath," spoke of the demonic calling of "the chosen one," and on "Shock Wave" from *Never Say Die!*, we return to the "chosen one." Despite the efficacy of love, occasional calls to God, and the embrace of life-giving occultist imagery, this remains a fatalistic universe: "There's no reason for you to run / You can't escape the fate of the chosen one." In imitation of biblical apocalyptic, Black Sabbath invokes images of red skies and rising moons as signs of the end. The chosen one will not only die, but now realizes it, as he is caught in time itself between worlds buffeted by wind, mist, cold, dulled senses, and evil forces. Despite the myriad of worlds, lives, calls to God, and visions of Satan, in the end the reality of death does not negate that we are chosen.

Thus, as young men recalling the seer on Patmos two millennia ago, Black Sabbath in their early albums wrapped together hope and fear, dream and nightmare to present what is seemingly a counter-intuitive view of the cosmos; or, if not counter-intuitive, a rewriting of a more ancient understanding of the dualism of the divine. As Ward describes it: "Sometimes we've felt that God could be Satan . . . God is neither good nor evil. There's some of the Devil, or Abraxas, in God. . . .

If he was supposed to be only good, we couldn't believe him."[19] Black Sabbath embraced the incongruities of life and religious faith to speak through images redolent of Christian apocalyptic hope for the marginalized. And while they were a commercial success, they were also a social flash point, upsetting Christians and Satanists alike.[20] In the end, Sabbath's songs, like all good apocalyptic art, offer a vision that transcends their time and place and disturbs the powers that be.[21]

Notes

1. Tony Iommi with T.J. Lammers, *Iron Man: My Journey Through Heaven and Hell with Black Sabbath* (Cambridge, MA: Da Capo, Press, 2011), 53–54, 56–57, 61, 67; Ian Christe, *Sound of the Beast: The Complete Headbanging History of Heavy Metal* (New York: itbooks, 2003), 4; Ozzy Osbourne with Chris Ayres, *I Am Ozzy* (New York: Grand Central Publishing, 2009), 82–83, 91, 96; and Robin Sylvan, *Traces of the Spirit: The Religious Dimensions of Popular Music* (New York: New York University Press, 2002), 156–157.

2. Black Sabbath, *Paranoid*, Liner Notes (Vertigo, Warner Bros., 1970), 2; Black Sabbath, *Greatest Hits 1970–1978* (Rhino, Warner Bros., 2006), 3; and W. Scott Poole, *Satan in America: The Devil We Know* (Lanham, MD: Rowman & Littlefield Publishers, Inc., 2009), 176.

3. Martin Popoff, *Black Sabbath: Doom Let Loose* (Toronto: ECW Press, 2006), 2–4; Martin Popoff, *Black Sabbath FAQ: All That's Left to Know on the First Name in Metal* (Milwaukee: Backbeat Books, 2011), 87–88; Helen Farley, "Demons, Devils and Witches: The Occult in Heavy Metal Music," in Gerd Bayer, ed., *Heavy Metal Music in Britain* (Surrey: Ashgate Publishing, 2009), 73–88. Iommi, 10–11; Osbourne, 5, 12–13; and Christe, 1.

4. "Black Sabbath: The Last Supper," dir. Jeb Brien and Monica Hardiman (Epic Music Video, 1999); Iommi, 82; Osbourne, 46–47; Popoff, *Black Sabbath FAQ*, 31.

5. Mike Stark, *Black Sabbath: An Oral History* (New York: Avon Books, 1998), 7, 9.

6. Iommi, 2, 81–82; Osbourne, 6; Christe, 9; Farley, 92–93; Nick Ravo, "AT TEA WITH: Ozzy Osbourne; Family Man. Fights Fat, Is Good With Kids," *The New York Times*, 23 September 1992, www.nytimes.com/1992/09/23/garden/at-tea-with-ozzy-osbourne-family-man-fights-fat-is-good-with-kids.html?pagewanted=all; and Popoff, *Black Sabbath: Doom Let Loose*, 7–8, 21, 60. Though Osbourne's upbringing included a nominally Catholic mother, his religious education came from the Church of England, Christe, 9.

7. Carl E. Braaten, "The Recovery of Apocalyptic Imagination," in Carl E. Braaten and Robert W. Jenson, eds., *The Last Things: Biblical and Theological Perspectives on Eschatology* (Grand Rapids, MI: William B. Eerdmans Publishing Company, 2002), 16–17.

8. Braaten, 26–29; and Elaine Pagels, *Revelations: Visions, Prophecy, and Politics in the Book of Revelation* (New York: Viking, 2012), Chapter 1.

9. Pagels, 34.

10. Christe, 2.

11. Iommi, 73; Christe, 9; Osbourne, 110; and Aleister Crowley, *Moonchild: A Prologue* (York Beach, ME: Samuel Weiser, Inc., 1970), 277–291.

12. Gerttrude Casanova, 'St. Walburga,' *The Catholic Encyclopaedia*, Vol. 15 (New York: Robert Appleton Company, 1912), www.new advent.org/cathen/15526b.htm (accessed 13 March 2012); and Ruth Edna Kelly, *The Book of Hallowe'en* (1919) (Charleston: Forgotten Books, 2012), 91–95, www.forgottenbooks.org/info/9781605069494.

13. Crowley, 280–282.

14. Pagels, 26.

15. This conception is not unlike that of Bono's eschatology articulated in U2's songs. Though there could be almost no more different bands to compare on this front, this mixture of sexuality, geopolitics, and personal suffering and salvation are similar. See, "Comic Endings: Spirit and Flesh in Bono's Apocalyptic Imagination, 1980–1983," in Michael J. Gilmour, ed., *Call Me the Seeker: Listening to Religion in Popular Music* (New York: Continuum, 2005), 61–78.

16. Consider also "Thrill of it All" from *Sabotage*.

17. Popoff, *Black Sabbath: Doom Let Loose*, 88.

18. Pagels, 17.

19. Popoff, *Black Sabbath: Doom Let Loose*, 24.

20. Pagels, 171, 177; and Popoff, *Black Sabbath: Doom Let Loose*, 24, 59–60.

21. Thanks to Michael Gilmour and Joseph Bongiorno for their helpful comments on an earlier draft of this chapter and the Centre for Studies in Religion & Society at the University of Victoria for its support.

Part II

PLAYING DEVIL'S ADVOCATE

Chapter 4

Black Sabbath and the Sound of Evil

Joel McIver

"What is this that stands before me?" wails Ozzy Osbourne at the beginning of the unholy trinity of heavy metal nomenclature, the song "Black Sabbath" on the album *Black Sabbath* by Black Sabbath. Whatever the "figure in black which points at me" was, it was nothing we ever wanted to meet. It was evil incarnate, we assumed. And we really didn't need the rest of the lyrics to know that. The music itself sounds evil, doesn't it?

Philosophers since Plato (428–328 BCE) have debated whether or not beauty is in the eye of the beholder, whether or not there are objective standards by which we can judge the merits of artworks. While Sabbath's artistic greatness is not a matter of debate among Sabbath's fans, it is a matter of debate among music fans more generally. And it's a matter of debate among philosophers whether the question even can have an objectively right answer. Since you're reading this book, though, it seems safe to assume that you don't need to be convinced as to Sabbath's greatness.[1] So let's consider a related question, what makes Sabbath's songs sound evil?

Sinister Sounds

Examples of their sinister sound are everywhere within the Sabbath canon: take a listen to the graveyard thump of the drums, sliding

Black Sabbath and Philosophy: Mastering Reality, First Edition. Edited by William Irwin.
© 2013 John Wiley & Sons, Inc. Published 2013 by John Wiley & Sons, Inc.

sneer of the guitars, and the guttural distortion of the vocals in the introduction to "Iron Man," for example. Consider also the eerie fade to near-silence 30 seconds into "Behind the Wall of Sleep," leavened only by that questioning guitar riff, the slightly queasy wah-wah guitars and descending chord sequence of "Electric Funeral," and, while we're on the subject of stomach-churning wah effects, how about Geezer Butler's creepy bass solo before the opening chords of "N.I.B."? Then there's the unsettling harmonica of "The Wizard," the thunderous build-up at the beginning of "Children of the Grave," and the first, unnerving seconds of "After Forever." Even the lovely acoustic melodies of classic Iommi solo pieces such as "Orchid" are pensive rather than optimistic, an indicator of the great man's winning way with a minor chord (of which we'll say more later).

Even among people who don't actually like Sabbath's songs, there's no disagreement about this malevolent sound. But what makes it sound evil? Music critics like me make a living by commenting on the speed, pitch, and dynamics of songs, aspects that can be gauged objectively, but the sound of evil is more elusive.

Ask Sabbath

Perhaps someone should ask the members of Black Sabbath about this. Surely they'll have the answer for us?

Sadly not: I contribute articles to a bunch of British and American rock magazines, and, over the last decade or so, I've had the pleasure of interviewing the original four members of Black Sabbath many times. While the guys who came along later, the late Ronnie James Dio among them, had highly sophisticated ideas about the nature of the music they were making, whenever I've asked Ozzy, Tony, Geezer, or Bill how they came up with the uniquely spooky sound of Sabbath's 1970s albums, I've always found their responses on the subject a bit deflating.

The truth is, none of them really know how they made their music sound so evil. They didn't know at the time, and they don't know now. Sure, they know what chords they played, and they know where the lyrics found their inspirations—but ask any of them abstract questions about how and why Sabbath's songs possessed nebulous qualities such as heaviness, scariness, and so on, and you'll get nowhere.

"Obviously that stuff came along with the band name," Geezer himself told me, "which we took from the first song we wrote together. Thank God it was that one, or we could have been called 'Fairies Wear Boots' . . . we just thought, we like this name, it sounds good. We didn't even think of any black magic connotations."[2]

Not only did the Sab Four create their music from a position where they didn't understand the significance of what they were doing—which is to say, simultaneously inventing heavy metal, doom metal, and arguably black metal—they had no choice but to do so. Thanks to the group's terrible socioeconomic background, glum worldview, limited skills, and dearth of opportunities, Black Sabbath's route was always likely to be into the darkness.

Black Sabbath's music definitely sounded evil but, at that point in their careers, the musicians neither knew nor cared *how* to make it sound that way: it just did. The press whipped up a storm of controversy that seems quaint by today's standards but which felt pretty damn apocalyptic at the time. Fans loved it. Even your friendly local witch coven loved it, with followers of various occult sects showing up to gigs in order to meet their heroes—who promptly retreated in terror, scared witless by the crazies who they'd inadvertently attracted.

All this excitement, however, was caused by a simple phenomenon—the function of human ears and the signals they send to the brain. We're talking here about psychoacoustics, the science of how our brains assign meaning to sound waves. While I'd love to point to the inherently "evil" sound of Black Sabbath's music and inform you that Satan himself resides within it, unfortunately I cannot.

Sure, I hear you say: music may not have intrinsically positive or negative qualities other than those we impose on it, but how come we all seem to agree that a given composition—say, "Iron Man"—sounds pretty damn scary?

Well, let me tell you.

Even though Sabbath's primary lyricist Geezer Butler deliberately chose to write about demonic subjects, his work would have been mocked roundly if the music, largely the product of Tony Iommi, hadn't sounded appropriately dark. Knowingly or otherwise, Iommi utilized several well-known tricks to create an evil effect. Want to know how he did it?

(Fretting) Hand of Doom

Tune your guitar to E, or more properly a conventional frequency called A440, and you'll be in conventional tuning. Tune lower than that, as many heavy metal groups choose to do, and you'll make a darker, doomier, "heavier" sound. Sabbath were probably the first band to do this, and they did it partly out of necessity and partly out of aesthetic intent. Here is how Iommi explained it to me:

> When I was a teenager, I was working in a factory on a machine which pressed sheet metal. I got my middle fingers on my right hand caught in it and, without thinking, I pulled them out quickly. The weight on them was so great that parts of those fingers stayed behind, down to the first joint on the middle finger and most of the way down to the joint on the ring finger. The nails were broken off and then surgically re-implanted. I had to work really hard to get round it. I had to play more simply: there were certain chords I couldn't play and some extensions I couldn't do. I had to think of ways of playing that were effective but still possible for me.[3]

Bad news for Iommi, great news for us—for this lower tuning made his riffs significantly heavier, or more evil-sounding, if you will. Now, there is some debate about when exactly Iommi first tuned low, but that he did it is beyond question.[4] He has repeatedly claimed to have tuned down as much as three semitones in order to sound heavier.[5] Lower frequencies always sound powerful and thus more threatening to the human ear, whether it's the rumble of thunder, the revving of a racecar engine, or the thud of hooves as a bison charges at us across the plains. Amplify those frequencies to ear-bleeding levels, as Sabbath routinely did when they played live, and you're a long way toward making a sound that will be interpreted as evil.

That's trick number one.

More significantly from a musicological and therefore a psychoa-coustic point of view, Iommi utilized a sinister interval in several of his songs that was guaranteed to fill listeners with fear. It's variously known as a tritone, a diminished fifth, or as the *diabolus in musica* or devil's interval: the first because it spans three whole tones, the second because the interval stops just short of a perfect fifth, and the last because it was thought by some medieval clerics and composers to reflect the malevolence of Satan. The last of these descriptors is obviously the most metal, so let's go with that one. In terms of how human ears interpret the devil's interval, the sense of unease it produces is due to its internal dissonance: when notes sound dissonant together, we get slightly spooked, and that's what makes it such a useful interval for heavy metal songwriting. In medieval times the interval was labeled "restless" or "unstable." For our purposes, we'll just call it evil. Because evilness is cool, let's face it.

The devil's interval has a long and distinguished history of unnerving people. Before 1600 or thereabouts, scholars of musical notation couldn't figure out a way to write it down, and because so much musical study was religious in nature, it followed that the tritone attracted the disapproval of the clerics who battled with it. Rumors abound to this day that the interval was actually banned by medieval authorities, but evidence of this is scarce, and furthermore, once musical tonality assumed a more modern, flexible form at the start of the seventeenth century, it became merely part and parcel of the musical vocabulary and thus less of a threat. Still, while the church may have relented, the tritone sounds pretty damn disturbing to this day.

As we've seen, Tony Iommi had no idea of all this dusty historical stuff when he used the devil's interval.[6] He just knew it sounded evil. The tritone has qualities that are unsettling, and so it isn't a great stretch to link it with the unsettling nature of evil. The most famous occurrence of the devil's interval in the Sabbath canon is in the song "Black Sabbath" itself. The slow, doomy majority of the song is a simple repetition of root note, plus octave, plus tritone. Unaccompanied, Iommi's guitar and Butler's bass sound sinister enough when playing this riff. But when Ozzy wails "Oh no, no, please God help me!" and the drums and thunder sound effects are added, the overall impression is that hell itself is being unleashed.

That's trick number two.

Here's a third. Whether you realize it or not, you have heard any number of horror movie soundtracks that include violins and violas. A common trick employed by soundtrack composers is to instruct the players of those instruments to execute fast tremolo strokes, bowing the strings back and forth rapidly, rather like a fly rubbing its forelegs together. This unsettling effect introduces tension into the music, never permitting the listener to relax fully: Iommi does this on the devil's interval in "Black Sabbath," to add the fear factor and to make the chords sound "bigger," as—thanks to that early industrial accident—he can only fret comfortably with two fingers.

"Going Through (Key) Changes . . ."

Any musician will tell you that major chords sound happy and minor chords sound sad. This is true, but minor chords can also sound oppressive or downright terrifying. A popular example from outside the Sabbath canon is Darth Vader's "Imperial March" from the *Star Wars* movie series. Most marches are written in a major key to encourage people to get up and march along, but the "Imperial March" is written in a minor key to make it frightening. Do *you* want to get up and march alongside Vader? Well, exactly.

Now, in heavy music there's a corollary to the "happy major, sad minor" rule, stating that it's possible to avoid utilizing either major or minor "sex" in chords simply by playing a power chord, the root-note-plus-fifth combination that you've heard anchoring a million rock and metal songs. A power chord allows the bass guitar or other accompanying instrument to move around in a related major or minor chord, thus setting the tone of the song. The sound of evil is therefore literally at the musicians' fingertips.

We should note, however, that minor keys don't always make songs sound sinister: minors can have an effect that is sad, contemplative, or thoughtful. It's also possible that someone accustomed to non-Western music (Indian ragas, say), might not feel the same emotional effect as a person who has listened to FM rock their whole life long.

The evilness of Sabbath's 1970s music didn't solely come from the guitars, of course. Ozzy Osbourne sang without the benefit of any voice training, as is to be expected from a musician of his background, and evolved a monotonous style that perfectly suited the atmosphere of the songs. He even failed to master the art of singing from the diaphragm, the technique most professional singers adopt because it adds power and sustain to their voices. Fans don't care about any of this, of course, because Ozzy's vocals are an integral part of the early sound—and because his untrained style somehow adds to the songs' oppressive nature.

Bill Ward, a highly underrated member of Black Sabbath for the group's entire career—who sadly may not be included on the new album—was a trained jazz drummer, with a distinctive swing feel in his parts. Whether due to his inexperience or a desire to add some groove to Sabbath's sound, in the early years Ward was often prone to dragging the beat for a microsecond or two for a dark, doomy feel that gave the songs enormous power. Listen to the famous staccato verse riffs in "War Pigs" for evidence, especially in live versions of the song.

Like Ozzy's naïve vocals, Ward's imprecise drum parts—at least on the very early albums—gave the music a sense of weight that would have been missing had the drummer been playing in perfect time. "We had that grogginess and awkwardness in the music," he told me, "and we had Ozzy's monolithic sound and Geezer's lyrics, which at that time were so different and contradictory."[7]

Grogginess, awkwardness, inexperience, monotony . . . all these artistic imperfections contributed to the sense of doom that lingered around Black Sabbath's music, over and above any deliberate tricks such as the devil's interval or writing in minor keys. As with horror and pornography, two filmic genres designed to elicit reactions from the viewer, a too-perfect execution can detract from the effectiveness of the artwork, because life itself is far from perfect. No matter what our skills, as humans we blunder through life in a heuristic manner, finding our path largely by chance and never fully attaining perfection, because we live in an imperfect universe. That is why Black Sabbath's music often felt real, genuine, and lifelike: it was as flawed as you or I.

Sabbath Matters

So now we can understand why Black Sabbath's music sounds evil. And combined with Geezer Butler's lyrics and the album artwork, which reached its sinister peak with the nightmare figures of *Sabbath Bloody Sabbath*, any other interpretation seems unreasonable.

The philosopher Arthur Schopenhauer (1788–1860) argued that music expresses universal feelings like joy, sadness, and anger in itself, without regard to context and motive. Schopenhauer would say the devil's interval is not a mere musical convention. He would say that it sounds naturally and universally like "discord" or "malice."[8] But I would argue that the devil's interval is simply a musical convention that Western music uses to express evil. Someone who had never heard any Western music might not interpret the devil's interval as sounding evil at all. Still, although the devil's interval is a musical convention, it's not purely arbitrary. In real life, evil actions are not accompanied by a musical score. But, as we've noted, the devil's interval has qualities that are unsettling, and so it isn't a great stretch to link them with the unsettling nature of evil. Particularly with Sabbath, once the tritone was paired with macabre and occult imagery and lyrics, the convention was set in such a way that it is now hard to take it as a convention any longer. Still, that's what it is.

With the help of Sabbath, we can hear the evil loud and clear, as we can feel the chill run down our spine. Sabbath takes us "through the centuries to supersonic years" into an evil realm. This power to transport us is why Black Sabbath matters, and always will matter.[9]

Notes

1. But if you do need to be convinced be sure to read Chapter 7 in this volume, "The Art of Black Sabbath: Aristotle Joins the Band."
2. Joel McIver, *Sabbath Bloody Sabbath* (London: Omnibus Press, 2006), 38.
3. Ibid., 13–14.
4. Martin Popoff says that the down-tuning started on *Master of Reality*. See his *Black Sabbath: Doom Let Loose* (Toronto: ECW Press, 2006), 57; Paul Wilkinson says that "Warning" from the debut album was the first song with down-tuning. See his *Rat Salad: Black Sabbath The Classic Years 1969–1975* (New York: Thomas Dunne Books, 2006), 51.
5. Hal Leonard, *Guitar World Presents The 100 Greatest Guitarists Of All Time* (Milwaukee: Hal Leonard Corporation, 2002), 8.
6. Although Geezer Butler says that the day before they wrote "Black Sabbath" he played the opening of Holst's "Mars," which would likely have been the source of Iommi's inspiration. See the *Classic Albums: Paranoid* DVD (Eagle Rock Entertainment, 2010).
7. McIver, 38.
8. For more on Schopenhauer, see Chapter 5 in this volume, "The Worst of All Possible Worlds: Schopenhauer Meets Sabbath."
9. Thanks to William Irwin for his invaluable input.

Chapter 5

The Worst of All Possible Worlds
Schopenhauer Meets Sabbath

James Heathers

Debates about musical genres are best reserved for teenagers and historians. Who else has the myopia required? Who else cares to determine when some arbitrary category of sound crossed some other arbitrary barrier of sound between two poorly defined points? Regardless, when "heavy metal" began is well-trodden ground for discussion. From a historical perspective, we might find a point where references to "heavy metal" began, the first crystallization of the term in print. Equally legitimately, though, perhaps it is a question of process. At one particular point in time a set of musical techniques, equipment or delivery appeared to define the genre. But! There is also the question of content. Perhaps some theme must be present, some idea? If so, how much of it? Is a single song enough, or do we require a whole album or a catalog of work? Or perhaps just a single moment?

There is no technically correct answer to all this silliness, and we should take great relief that it doesn't matter. The truth is that artists don't usually define genres when art is made, and as a consequence the entire process of naming what their work represents is totally retrospective. (This is also a process that artists have a habit of rejecting when they see the labels others assign to them.) It seems enough to say that the first heavy metal band is whatever we agree it is now. Looking back over the historical record we might name:

Black Sabbath and Philosophy: Mastering Reality, First Edition. Edited by William Irwin.
© 2013 John Wiley & Sons, Inc. Published 2013 by John Wiley & Sons, Inc.

- the first band to play with sufficient live amplification to be "heavy" (Deep Purple, Blue Cheer);
- the first band to use the lyric "heavy metal" (Steppenwolf);
- the first band to be described in print as "heavy metal" (depending on who you believe—Sir Lord Baltimore, Alice Cooper, or Judas Priest);
- the first true occult album (Black Widow, Coven).

(This is to say nothing of the bevy of bands with some uncommonly heavy songs sprinkled through their catalogs—The Beatles, Cream, Led Zeppelin, Jimi Hendrix—or those who were playing in the late sixties with the development of distortion—The Kinks, for instance—or the swollen ranks of obscure rock and psychedelic bands that contained just enough of all of the above to earn the title of "proto-metal.")

Let us discard this whole debate now as an intellectual exercise. Heavy metal may have complicated roots at its base, but it is a living art, and this allows us to ask ... well, living artists. When we do that, the opinions of those who presently play heavy metal, our gatekeepers and lords and masters, allow no latitude or argument. There is only one original heavy metal band and it is Black Sabbath. Other bands might have been there at the time, but they can be relegated to a lesser category, "bands who knew Black Sabbath."

In a more academic essay, I might reference this remark heavily, but it is so readily apparent and is an opinion formed over such a long period of time as to defy footnotes. Watch any documentary, any interview with any modern heavy metal band (indeed simply find the nearest person with long hair and a faded *Coma of Souls* patch on their jacket) and it will just add to the chorus—Sabbath, Sabbath, Sabbath. They are our liturgy, our price of admission, and they are the taproot from which the tree of fantasy, absolution, and anger in music sprang, what heavy metal *is*, regardless of what it was.

This chapter is concerned with why this is the case, and with quite a peculiar explanation. Even a cursory familiarity with the circumstances under which Black Sabbath started reveals the most unlikely of events. From the worst of conditions, from the lowest of places, they rose meteorically even by the standards of an era of rock 'n roll replete with king-makers and overnight successes. The details of this rise are quite extraordinary and bear examination.

One Shot at Glory

Black Sabbath came from nowhere at all. Aston, Birmingham, England in the 1960s was the kind of place a time traveler with a sick sense of humor would drop someone for whom they had a moderate distaste. It was the kind of place Kurt Vonnegut would use to kill off a minor character, "just grey skies and corner pubs and sickly looking people who worked like animals on assembly lines."[1] Birmingham was an industrial town, the center of British Spitfire manufacture during World War II, and as a consequence it was bombed without mercy in the same manner as Coventry and Liverpool. Pictures of the sixties still show both the scars—husks of buildings which were never rebuilt—and the reason for them, the heavy industry that remained after the war. The landscape was tenements, industrial buildings, slag furnaces, and mills. Factories and foundries were the overwhelming centers of employment; Birmingham was one of those places where everyone worked in a factory. As Ozzy saw it, the ways out were simple: the factories, emigration, burglary, the military, or death.

(Or, of course, one could always become a rock star—the very idea, though! As Ozzy said, it was "one of those impossible things, like becoming an astronaut or a stuntman, or shagging Elizabeth Taylor."[2])

But The Beatles stood as undeniable evidence that four young lads from an industrial town could go from nowhere to everywhere, so four young men from Birmingham decided to try what had previously worked in Liverpool. From early fragmented efforts, a kind of haggard, driving hybrid blues emerged—a lot faster, a lot louder, but the blues nonetheless. The traditional music of the disenfranchised and the downtrodden was not enough, though. So eventually, the music turned toward the sinister. Some of the audience were scared, some wondered if the band was actually satanic. Far from it—it was just rock 'n roll to them. They loved the theatrics and unbridled escapism of iron monsters crushing the unworthy with leaden feet, of figures floating over lakes of fire and sulfur. Ozzy would later call "all the satanic stuff" a good source of "endless free publicity."[3]

Thus "Black Sabbath," the first plodding, sinister song that came to name the band, was not born of a deep malice fomented in the depths of the occult. Nothing so malevolent. The riffs sounded kind of grim, and the guys thought it would be fun to scare people, and people seemed to want to be scared. It just seemed to fit, somehow. (And of course, Led Zeppelin were heavy, but Sabbath wanted to be heavier. Boys will be boys.) This song they'd written seemed to capture the center of . . . something. None of the band mates were sure of quite what, though.

But regardless, the song came to name the band, and the band acquired some fledgling management, and they got to cut an album (self-titled, of course). *Black Sabbath* was recorded in a day. By today's standards, this might as well be the speed of light. It was mostly played live, mostly single tracked, almost 40 minutes of it. The band had no input into the final mix, mastering, or album art—they just tore out a day's worth of what essentially amounted to live tracks, and then they got back in the van.

The album did not meet with critical approval. Not a great deal of trade press survives from the period, but the band recall exclusively bad reviews. No less than Lester Bangs and Robert Christgau are both on record as hating the first Black Sabbath album. Bangs was scathing. As far as he was concerned, the lead guitar "dribbled wooden Claptonisms" and the vocals sounded akin to "Vanilla Fudge paying doggerel tribute to Aleister Crowley." Sabbath sounded "just like Cream! But worse."[4]

If even possible, Robert Christgau was more negative. He gave the album a C–, a grade that might be passing in other circumstances. But consider the fact that a few years later Christgau would give Lou Reed's *Metal Machine Music*—more than an hour of continuous, dense, baffling, and utterly alienating distortion, an album that borders on completely unlistenable, even after the popularization of genres of experimental and noise music, and one that Reed himself won't admit to listening to—a C+.[5]

But Against All Odds …

As would not be expected, Black Sabbath's success was ferocious and immediate. The debut album sold and sold, charting in the UK and then in the US. *Paranoid*, the second album recorded very soon afterward, did even better. Its release had to be delayed in the US, though, as it was thought that having two albums charting at the same time would drive down sales. What a problem to have! Sabbath's fledgling management were soon completely overwhelmed by the success, and the band immediately traded up (without worrying about any such niceties as contracts). This was eventually their downfall—after five albums (all platinum or multi-platinum), a few short years later, they had achieved the rock 'n roll trifecta, the one that waits at the end of any poorly managed period of impossible success: personal and creative destruction, popular success beyond all reasonable degree, and complete penury, making bad albums to afford to stand still and pay lawyers.

Thus, our question: *why them*? Certainly, there may be a handful of more improbable success stories. But the ability to define a whole genre, especially one that has such a visceral and widespread appeal, requires special attention. It is a truism that bands who start out trying to "redefine a genre" never do. Self-consciousness has no place in the space required to produce meaning from sounds that no one has ever heard before. The acute awareness of all that has preceded you forms an unavoidable obstacle to the truly new. For the beginning of a movement, we search for something inexpressible—a center that may exist in a whole album, or a single song, or even a single progression.

For Those Who Sow in Flames, an Explanation

To explain the meaning of this, we make the most curious of left turns, to the German philosopher Arthur Schopenhauer (1788–1860), whose work allows the most extraordinary freedom to explore the idea behind the phenomenon of Black Sabbath. Why so curious a turn? We shall see.

As might be expected for a man in whom we might grasp the roots of an art that revolves around distortion and discontent, Schopenhauer was resolutely grim. In his central work, *The World as Will and Representation*, he posed a profound division between the world of our day-to-day reality, what we generally perceive, or what our senses apprehend—Representation—and an altogether more massive Will—an unindividuated, metaphysical force of nature that was objectified in the world. Representations are the tip of an iceberg peeking from a striving, unknowable ocean of Will. Of course, Schopenhauer is not alone in such a conception of a powerful undercurrent of reality—the Greeks already had *eros*, and later Freud (who would read Schopenhauer at the height of his popularity) would have the *id*.

Schopenhauer would have understood Aston, Birmingham, 1969. He would have regarded the place as a colossal testament to the grotesqueries of the Will, a monument to this ceaseless unsatisfied striving, every inch of it alive and thrashing around to satisfy (and create) the problem of want: making new metals, new cars, new machine parts, industrial and consumer goods for a world that would never be happy with the amount they had. When Schopenhauer is described as a pessimist, this is not a reference to his character (although he most assuredly was a pessimist in that sense as well), but to his philosophy. Schopenhauer is a pessimist in the sense that he thought reality itself, in the service of the Will, is a horrible business. The fabric of reality itself denies happiness, fulfillment, and satisfaction. We live in the worst of all possible worlds. Schopenhauer would have regarded dropping dead on a factory floor in your fifties to be no different from any other demise, an inevitability and the ultimate achievement of life.

According to Schopenhauer, release from the clutches of the Will (assuming you stay alive for it, of course) comes either not at all, from self-denial ... or from music. Schopenhauer placed the music of his day on the highest pedestal, higher than all the other arts that allowed us to peek behind the veil of Representation at the true nature of reality. This is hardly "start a band, make it big, and leave town," though.

To Schopenhauer, while the other arts "speak only of shadows" that lie behind the wall of Representation, music maps much more directly onto the Will itself. With no obfuscation at all, music speaks of "joy, pain, sorrow, horror, gaiety, merriment, peace of mind *themselves*, to a certain extent in the abstract, their essential nature, without accessories."[6] So music allows us to experience these emotions and feelings in pure from. This is a wonderful and grandiose claim, but would this kind of pedestal pose any problem for the new music made by our boys from Aston? Not at all. Music had existed in its essential forms for far longer than any theories about it, and nothing was required for its comprehension and enjoyment. In many ways, Schopenhauer considered it to be totally unnecessary to take the notes and "clothe them in imagination." The notes themselves were enough. Black Sabbath, who simply made music that felt right, would agree entirely.

And what of the nature of heavy metal itself? Schopenhauer drew some particular analogies between the music of his time and the voices of component reality—bass tones of inorganic nature, tenor voices of animal kingdoms, and over it all, the speaking voice that apprehended singular essences of humanity itself. But the analogy goes even further. He understands notes, defined by immovable laws of physics as precise frequencies of vibration, as having natural consonance and dissonance. If you had ever asked him, Schopenhauer would have known immediately what musical interval to use if your world screamed out to you to write a song replete with morbidity—the diminished fifth.

The Original *Diabolus in Musica*

The diminished fifth is Sabbath's center of sonic fiendishness, the father of their sound. The precise division of an octave into two equal intervals of six semitones produces a primal dissonance known as the tritone, the original *diabolus in musica*. In Schopenhauer's system, lifted from Rameau (an eighteenth-century musical theorist) and Pythagoras (570–490 BCE), simple relations between notes were expressed in small numbers.[7] Thus, while a third is neat (5/3 of an octave), and a fifth neater still (3/2), a tritone is numerically hideous—either 45/32 or 64/45, depending on the source of its calculation.

Of course, this is romanticizing it somewhat, playing into the traditional seriousness that accompanies occult themes. It's not as if this musical system is correct (the physics goes a great deal deeper than these simple ratios), or that every Sabbath song relies on a palpable sense of evil. But "Black Sabbath," the song that started it all, makes ample use of the tritone. Classical music (at least, from the Romantic era onwards) and contemporary heavy metal are both soundly marinated in tritone tension. Even just choosing from works that open with the interval nakedly exposed we have several prime examples. Liszt's *Dante Sonata*, for instance, begins with three simple Andante steps through this interval, a reflection of the descent of Virgil and Dante into hell. The same interval dominates the colossal, buzzy, gruesome introduction to Massacre's "Dawn of Eternity" (1991), some of the very first true American death metal. Two more unlikely bedfellows could scarcely be imagined, but their intent is identical.

The interval's intemperate menace easily crosses the divide between musical styles, even in the same song. It is used to evoke a building sense of menace at the start of Holst's "Mars, Bringer of War," a wonderfully bold and brassy march over an insistent timpani beat that was borrowed wholesale for Nile's brutal death metal classic "Ramses Bringer of War" (1998)—the Egyptian equivalent of the Roman original, it might be supposed.[8] Holst's menacing introduction is heard almost in full, an accompaniment to a penetrating wall of building guitars that gives way into one of the most sonically dense pieces of music recorded in the twentieth century. The unbridled ferocity is centered around the use of a seven-string guitar, with the lowest string dropped to A, the death metal equivalent of Wagner writing for a colossally expanded orchestra complete with octobass, anvils, and thunder machine.

These musical works are all built around the same interval that came to *mean* Black Sabbath—a physically defined manifestation of anger and discontent. A voice that no one else had managed to execute, the first to ferment fantasy, horror, death, war, alienation, and fury. This raises a question that we can now handle easily—why was that so necessary in 1969?

Simply put, Aston was not Haight-Ashbury.[9] Hippies often forget that they were largely an American middle-class phenomenon and that they had very little traction in much of the rest of the world. While they wore flowers in their hair, great swathes of the world resented them with their space and freedom to "do your own thing." This was not reality in Aston, much in the same way "Morning in America" was a puerile dream to the hardcore punks from dirt-poor working class America in the 1980s.[10]

They are in this sense ideally suited, our prickly German philosopher and our angry, English faux-mystics, to explain why heavy metal started when it did, to explain the purity of the message Black Sabbath created. It is sometimes necessary to separate an author from their historical era or personality. But this is not one of those times, because there is an irony to our interpretation so far that cannot be lost here ...

Some Final Seeds of Hate

Schopenhauer would have *loathed* Black Sabbath and their music. And no doubt he would have taken the most violent exception to this chapter. Let us put to one side the man's pathological hatred of noise (he devoted an entire essay to the subject),[11] and his simultaneously elitist yet somewhat amateurish conception of how music should be constructed (he would have reserved his plaudits for far greater talents than a band who used to rent a practice space under a freeway bypass). The band's reaction to success would have set Schopenhauer's teeth on edge.

For a world crying out for musical relief, Black Sabbath produced reflections of the Will previously unheard. But then the band succumbed to the worst and most extreme excesses of the Will itself. Instead of keeping wants and desires at bay via self-denial and asceticism, Black Sabbath tried to smother the Will to death in a sea of lager, hash, cocaine, and women. What could that possibly result in but more desire, more want? Schopenhauer may have had a point. When the wheels fell off the wagon in the mid-1970s, after a meteoric rise with little to show for it, Sabbath may have wondered what the purpose of it all was. Perhaps the great pessimist was right. Perhaps this is the worst of all possible worlds.

Notes

1. *I Am Ozzy* (New York: Grand Central Publishing, 2010), 6.
2. Ibid., 30.
3. Ibid., 100.
4. Bangs' whole assault can be seen in the Rolling Stone archive: www.rollingstone.com/music/albumreviews/black-sabbath-19700917.
5. Christgau, unlike Bangs, never had a positive word to say about any Black Sabbath album … ever. All his collected reviews are available on-line here: www.robertchristgau.com/get_artist.php?name=Black+Sabbath.
6. *The World As Will and Idea*, trans. J. Kemp and R.B. Haldane: http://archive.org/stream/theworldaswillan01schouoft#page/338/mode/2up/search/joy.
7. Any modern book on the physics of music will be more accurate than the nineteenth-century conception of course.

8. Geezer Butler says that a day before they wrote the song "Black Sabbath" he played the opening of Holst's "Mars," which would likely have been the source of Iommi's inspiration. See the *Classic Albums*: *Paranoid* DVD (Eagle Rock Entertainment, 2010).

9. Haight-Ashbury was the spiritual center of the hippie movement, a district in San Francisco which was the center of the "Summer of Love." Their sentiments often didn't travel. Ozzy describes listening to the jukebox: "… All of a sudden, you'd hear all this hippy crap about 'gentle people' going to love-ins at Haight-Ashbury, whatever the fuck Haight-Ashbury was. Who gave a dog's arse about what people were doing in San Francisco, anyway?," *I Am Ozzy*, 46.

10. Watch the documentary "American Hardcore" to see Vic Bondi (the singer from Articles of Faith) articulate this at a volume that convincingly describes the situation.

11. Yes, noise. The man was a professional elitist and an unbearable snob: "It is obvious, therefore, that here we have to do with an act of pure wantonness; nay, with an impudent defiance offered to those members of the community who work with their heads by those who work with their hands. That such infamy should be tolerated in a town is a piece of barbarity and iniquity, all the more as it could easily be remedied by a police-notice to the effect that every lash shall have a knot at the end of it. There can be no harm in drawing the attention of the mob to the fact that the classes above them work with their heads, for any kind of headwork is mortal anguish to the man in the street." From: http://ebooks.adelaide.edu.au/s/schopenhauer/arthur/pessimism/chapter8.html.

Chapter 6

Tony Iommi's Hand of Doom
From Plastic Fingertips to Creative Freedom

Ken Pepper

On his final day of work in a sheet metal factory in his native Birmingham, England, 17-year-old Tony Iommi lost the tips of the middle and ring fingers on his right hand (his fretting hand, since Iommi is a lefty) in an industrial accident. At first he thought he would never play again, but after a brief and unsuccessful attempt at playing right-handed, Iommi eventually relearned to play guitar using homemade prosthetic fingertips made from bits of plastic bottles. Iommi's "never say die" attitude (sorry, couldn't resist) led him to adapt his playing style to accommodate his injury, and the rest is rock history.

Still, we may wonder, how does Iommi experience the plastic tips when he performs? Is he conscious of them as an intermediary obstacle between his right hand and his instrument? How can he play with two fingertips he can't feel? Furthermore, was his creative freedom stifled, enhanced, or completely unaffected by his injury? Perhaps surprisingly, Maurice Merleau-Ponty's (1908–1961) classic philosophical text, *Phenomenology of Perception*, can help us in answering these questions.

The Phenomenology of Minds, Bodies, and Little Bits of Plastic

Merleau-Ponty was part of a movement in twentieth-century philosophy called Phenomenology, founded by the German philosopher Edmund

Black Sabbath and Philosophy: Mastering Reality, First Edition. Edited by William Irwin.
© 2013 John Wiley & Sons, Inc. Published 2013 by John Wiley & Sons, Inc.

Husserl (1859–1938). Phenomenologists believed that we can only make sense of philosophical problems about perception, freedom, knowledge, and the relationship between mind and body if we first get clear about how we consciously experience these things. Phenomenology set itself the modest yet tricky task of producing pure descriptions of experience. The idea was to describe conscious experience on its own terms before it gets interpreted by philosophical or scientific theories. Merleau-Ponty held that this can only be done by understanding the way we perceive the world, and that perception can only be understood if we pay close attention to how the body structures perceptual experience. For Merleau-Ponty, to be conscious and to be embodied are not things we can understand in isolation from each other. Rather, they are two sides of the same philosophical coin.

Historically, philosophy and its younger cousin, psychology, have struggled to know what to make of the body. René Descartes (1596–1650), reflecting on the nature of knowledge in *Meditations on First Philosophy*, famously argued he could doubt the existence of his body but he could never doubt the existence of his mind. Descartes reasoned that in theory he could be misled about the existence of his body because it is part of the "external" world. This is the world that exists outside of the mind, and that can only be known through our senses, which can be misled or deceived. But Descartes couldn't doubt the existence of his mind, because in order to doubt it, he'd have to think. So the very act of doubting proves the mind's existence! Hence his famous *cogito ergo sum*—"I think therefore I am." The picture inherited from Descartes is still very influential today. Even contemporary psychologists, neuroscientists, and artificial intelligence engineers often talk of conscious minds as though they were hidden away in people's heads, with bodily movements as the outer effects of inner mental causes. Merleau-Ponty dedicates much of *Phenomenology of Perception* to arguing against this Cartesian conception of the body as external to the mind, which he calls the "objective" conception of the body. If we only think of the body objectively, then we can't make sense of how we perceive and interact with things in the world around us, because this way of thinking fails to pay attention to what human experience is actually like. Here is where Tony Iommi's case can be instructive. If the body is understood merely as an external object, then guitar playing consists of a linear series of causally related events beginning with private inner thoughts and culminating in acts of fretting and picking. On this view, Iommi's plastic fingertips are simply extra bits of material stuff involved in a causal series stretching from his premotor cortex to his signature Gibson SG. But is this really the only way, let alone the correct way, to understand what's going on?

From a guitarist's point of view, what's happening when they play? Do they have to consciously think about their movements, plan them in advance, and then execute an action to produce an intended effect? Anyone with a modicum of guitar-playing experience (which, dear readers, I'm guessing many of you have) knows that this is not the case. Only complete novices, or perhaps more experienced players trying to learn a new song or technique, have to plan their fingering in advance, pay close attention to the spatial location of frets and strings, or attend to their individual actions at all, really. For the expert player, uppicking, downpicking, fretting, hammering-on, pulling-off, sliding, vibrato, chord changes, palm muting, and so on all happen naturally and effortlessly, and are experienced as a flowing whole rather than a series of distinct thoughts, decisions, movements, and perceptions. But the objective conception of the body tempts us to think that it must be right, that Tony Iommi must be doing something extra, because he has additional bits of equipment (his plastic fingertips) to attend to when he frets strings. However, Merleau-Ponty's phenomenological account of the body shows us why this isn't quite right.

How do Tony Iommi's plastic fingertips fit with these phenomenological observations about guitar playing? Since the plastic fingertips are wedged in between the fingers on his right hand and his guitar neck, does Iommi's tactile perception stop short of the fret board? Viewed from the outside, we might say that he senses the tips with his actual fingers, but not the fret board itself. And certainly the tips themselves don't sense anything! But if the tips were experienced like this, then they would be an obstacle to Iommi's playing; they would get in the way of his perceptual access to his instrument. If the only way to understand Iommi's experience were based on the objective conception of the body, he would be forced to play like a perpetual beginner, keeping track of his plastic fingertips by either constantly looking at them, or by estimating the location of the tips by feeling them with his damaged fingers and inferring their location relative to the fret board using an estimate of their size and shape. This would be rather a lot to keep track of! In any case, I've seen Iommi play live twice (with both Ozzy- and Dio-era lineups of Sabbath, I'm very proud to say), and he definitely doesn't do this!

In order to make sense of what it's really like for Iommi to play with his plastic fingertips, we have to follow Merleau-Ponty in understanding the body not just as an object, but also as it is experienced. Once we get clear on the phenomenology of the body, then we will be equipped to think about how the plastic tips figure in Iommi's experience. We hardly ever experience our own bodies as objects with a separate existence from our minds. We feel sensations in our bodies, and we can move them from the inside at will. What is more, all our perceptions are related to our body in one way or another. This gives us our perspective on objects. Things look large or small, near or far, usable or unusable relative to the shape, size, location, and abilities of our bodies. When we move at will, we don't experience an inner mental world on one side of us and an outer material world on the other. In contrast to the objective body, Merleau-Ponty calls this phenomenological (first-person, experiential, lived) conception of the body the "phenomenal body."[1]

The phenomenal body has a flexible structure. Pick up a cup from your coffee table. Without trying, your fingers will configure themselves around the cup, as though your arm and hand were anticipating what's about to happen. These aren't things you choose to do. They are, rather, things that happen automatically whenever you do do something you choose to do. At every point during the movement you'll have an implicit awareness of where the rest of your body is. Asked where your arm is in relation to the rest of your body, you'll be able to say immediately. All of this can still work without the need to look where any of your body parts are. Your conscious experience of moving, acting, and sensing is structured by the sort of body you have. This is what Merleau-Ponty means when he says "my body is wherever there is something to be done."[2] He called this ordered structure of the phenomenal body the *body schema*.

Without the body schema, we'd have no perspective, no way to immediately distinguish our own bodies from other things around us, and no sense of what sorts of actions we're capable or incapable of doing at will prior to testing them out. Before moving a limb or judging the distance between ourselves and something on the other side of a room, we'd have to visually check where our bodies were. We don't need to do this, because the schematic structure of the phenomenal body does all the hard work for us. Only when something goes badly wrong, as happens with some neurological impairments, do we need to check where our bodies are before acting, or need to use evidence to work out which thing we are. Hence Merleau-Ponty has Descartes in his sights when he writes, "Consciousness is not in the first place a matter of 'I think' but of 'I can'."[3]

Following Merleau-Ponty, we can better understand Iommi's experience by considering the plastic tips as incorporated into his body schema and extending his phenomenal body. From Iommi's point of view, in order to play as proficiently as he does, the plastic tips must stop being things he perceives and become things he perceives *with*. Phenomenologically speaking, the tips aren't extra bits of equipment, but another part of his body through which he directly perceives his guitar.

Phenomenology of Perception is littered with examples of similar body schema extensions. Consider the case of a blind man who learns to feel his way around with a stick. When we think objectively, we know that the impact of the end of the man's stick on the ground causes motion in the stick that stimulates the surface of his hand, which causes an electrochemical signal to be sent to the primary somatosensory cortex in his brain, which is then processed and interpreted as coming from the spatial point in front of him. But, phenomenologically, his experience is nothing like this. The end of the stick is "an area of sensitivity."[4] He doesn't need to work out where the stick is, or that the rock he's poking with it is small, hard, and about three feet away. The man is dimly aware of the length and location of the stick in the same way in which he is dimly aware of the length and location of his own arm, but it is not an object of perception for him in the same way the rock on the ground is. Rather, once he's picked up the habit of using the stick in this way he quite literally perceives the rock through it, as though he had a temporarily extended body schema. (You can try this for yourself.) Merleau-Ponty has a nice way of putting the point, "once the stick has become a familiar instrument, the world of feelable things recedes and now begins, not at the outer skin of the hand, but at the end of the stick."[5]

Like the blind man's walking stick, Iommi's plastic fingertips temporarily extend his body schema, allowing him to play smoothly and accurately. Because he's accustomed to using the tips every time he plays, he doesn't need to pay special attention to them or his right hand. In fact, if he did, it would probably mess up his playing, because he'd be back in the beginner's boat of paying close attention to each movement he makes and planning the next one in advance. And if you're still not convinced, think of it this way: it's really no different in principle from what's going on in his picking hand! Guitar picks aren't (objective) body parts, but guitarists are able to sense the locations of the strings through them with ease, usually without looking. Once they've acquired the skill (the "perceptual habit," as Merleau-Ponty would call it), when they play the "world of feelable things" really does begin at the end of the guitar pick, not their thumb and forefinger. This capacity to temporarily incorporate objects into the body schema is one of the main things separating experienced pickers from beginners. All guitarists extend their body schema in one way or another (unless they only ever finger pick). Iommi is just a very special case.

So, are Tony Iommi's plastic fingertips parts of his body, or are they just bits of stuff in the external world? The answer is that they're only bits of stuff in the external world if his entire body is too, that is, if we think of the body just as the objective body. Viewed phenomenologically (that is, when we focus on the experience itself), this view is just plain wrong and cannot help us understand what it's like for Iommi to use his plastic tips or the way he perceives his guitar. As Merleau-Ponty notes, "it is never our objective body that we move, but rather our phenomenal body."[6] Iommi's plastic fingertips, just like the picks of other (as a rule, far less awesome) guitarists, become part of the schematic structure of the phenomenal body, and this is how we should understand his consciousness of playing.

Tony Iommi's Creative Freedom and the Birth of Heavy Metal

Though fellow Brits Led Zeppelin and Deep Purple may have set the scene, Black Sabbath was the first bona fide heavy metal band. So it's really no exaggeration to say that, as the band's primary composer, Tony Iommi pretty much invented metal. And he did it all with two damaged fingers that restrict his playing. Does Iommi's minor disability limit his creative freedom? Or does the fact that he overcame his injury show that it has no bearing on his freedom at all?

In the final chapter of *Phenomenology of Perception*, Merleau-Ponty argues that to understand what it means to be free, we need to get rid of the popular understanding of this issue as a clash between intentions, desires, and free choices on the one hand, and limitations imposed from the external world on the other. To understand what it is for human beings to be free, we need to understand how we can *both* be in a body that restricts what we can do *and* yet be able to act of our own free will. Tony Iommi would have made a great case study for Merleau-Ponty, because the creative freedom he achieved by honing his playing style was partly due to the restrictions placed on him by the injury to his right hand. His frequent use of two-finger powerchords, box-shaped minor pentatonic scales, and his tendency to move further up the neck while staying on the bottom strings rather than playing the same notes further down the neck on higher strings (resulting in a fuller, thicker sound, which is a very popular technique in modern metal), are all integral parts of his signature sound that are due in part to his limited range of movement. But Iommi also came up with all sorts of other musical innovations purely for the sake of sounding ever heavier, like pioneering high gain amplification, and using drop tunings.[7] Both Iommi's bodily limitations and his over-arching musical vision contribute equally to the Sabbath sound, and both originate in Iommi's capacity to exercise his creative freedom. This supports Merleau-Ponty's point that "there is [. . .] never determinism and never absolute choice, I am never a thing and never bare consciousness."[8] Freedom is not the all or nothing affair philosophers have often supposed it to be.

If we think of Iommi's creative freedom as being completely stifled by the damage to his fretting hand, then the Sabbath sound and the metal genre (and subsequent subgenres) it inspired was all a lucky accident that resulted from him making the only sort of music he possibly could, given his unfortunate circumstances. This is just silly. Iommi did, after all, *decide* to start playing again, *choose* what kind of music he wanted to make (scary, heavy, and loud), and *create* a new sound by writing the sorts of songs he thought were right for Sabbath. Perhaps his injury didn't limit his freedom at all, then? In *Being and Nothingness*, Merleau-Ponty's one-time pal Jean-Paul Sartre (1905–1980) (they had a nasty falling out over politics, as twentieth-century French philosophers were prone to do), claimed that human beings are *radically* free because we always choose the attitude we take toward any situation we find ourselves in, even when we don't realize we're choosing it ("Not to choose is, in fact, to choose not to choose").[9] Though we always find ourselves thrown into a certain situation (which, for Sartre, includes being in a certain place, at a certain time, with a certain sort of body), this doesn't limit our freedom to choose the attitude we take toward this situation and thereby decide its meaning for ourselves, thereby making ourselves into what we are. According to Sartre, even disabilities don't limit freedom because we can always choose the significance they have for us,

> [. . .] We are a choice, and for us, to choose is to choose ourselves. Even this disability which I suffer I have assumed by the very fact that I live; I surpass it toward my own projects. I make of it the very obstacle of my being, and I cannot be crippled without choosing myself as crippled. This means I choose the way in which I constitute my disability as "unbearable", "humiliating", "to be hidden", "to be revealed to all", "an object of pride", "the justification for my failures", *etc.*[10]

If Sartre is right (and the last chapter of *Phenomenology of Perception* is dedicated to showing he's not), then Iommi's freedom was unchanged after his accident, because even though he lost two fingertips, his ability to choose the attitude toward his minor disability remained unaffected. But this isn't right either. Whatever attitude he freely takes toward his damaged fingers, if his plastic tips fall off, Iommi's hardly able to play at all (and only in great pain). And before he grew accustomed to the plastic fingertips, his playing would have been clumsy and inaccurate compared to how it was before his accident. So he *has* been deprived of certain possibilities for action that he once had. Also, Iommi has to use extra thin gauge guitar strings because fretting regular strings is virtually impossible for him. This makes staying in tune trickier—another obstacle caused by changes to his situation beyond his control. More importantly, it was only because of a chance encounter with a record by two-fingered jazz guitarist Django Reinhardt, played to him by his former manager from the factory, that Iommi was inspired to relearn to play at all. It is wrongheaded to insist, as Sartre would, that Iommi was always free to refuse his disability, transcend his predicament, and relearn to play. Playing again was not a "live" possibility for Iommi until Reinhardt's story showed him it was possible. As Merleau-Ponty emphasizes, freedom is not a matter of choosing to accept or refuse your situation, but of responding to the possibilities that your particular situation affords. And some possibilities are more "live" than others, depending on how the rest of your life turns out.

My actual freedom is not on the hither side of my being, but before me, in things. We must not say that I continually choose myself, on the excuse that I *might* continually refuse what I am. Not to refuse is not the same thing as to choose.[11]

Iommi's monumental creative achievement (the invention of metal) is, in a sense, no more or less remarkable for having been the product of a man missing the tips of two fingers. Only Tony Iommi could have invented metal. Not because he was forced to by external factors causing him to be unfree to do otherwise, nor because he has the radical freedom to be continually "born again" (pun very much intended) just by choosing his attitudes, but because only Iommi, by taking up *his* possibilities for action, which are determined by *his* body being in *his* situations, could have exercised his own distinctive creative freedom in that exact way.

Notes

1. Hence the joke I once told a colleague working on a Ph.D. on Merleau-Ponty: Q. Why was Merleau-Ponty so popular with the ladies? A. He had a phenomenal body.
2. Maurice Merleau-Ponty, *Phenomenology of Perception* (London: Routledge, 2002), 291.
3. Ibid., 159.
4. Ibid., 165.
5. Ibid., 175–176.
6. Ibid., 121.
7. Side note: It's sometimes claimed that Iommi tuned down to slacken his guitar strings to put less pressure on his injured fingers. This isn't quite true. Both *Black Sabbath* and *Paranoid* were recorded entirely in standard tuning, and although the band did play live in Eb as early as 1970, this was primarily for the sake of Ozzy's voice. The later use of D and C# tunings was purely for the sake of heaviness. Iommi's primary way of dealing with the difficulty of fretting with his damaged fingers was to use lighter gauge strings, which put less pressure on his fingertips while fretting. Martin Popoff says that the down-tuning started on *Master of Reality*. See his *Black Sabbath: Doom Let Loose* (Toronto: ECW Press, 2006), 57.

8. Merleau-Ponty, 527.
9. Jean-Paul Sartre, *Being and Nothingness* (London: Routledge, 2007), 503.
10. Ibid., 352.
11. Merleau-Ponty, 526.

Part III
THE DARK ART OF METAL

Chapter 7

The Art of Black Sabbath
Aristotle Joins the Band

Greg Littmann

Black Sabbath, and heavy metal bands in general, suffer from a lot of misconceptions. Ignorant people will tell you that Black Sabbath (and all other metal bands) worship Satan, promote violence with their music, and even try to convince teenagers to commit suicide. But the strangest myth about the music of Black Sabbath, and about heavy metal in general, is that it has no value as art. Black Sabbath's early albums were reviled by music critics at the time of their release, even though they sold millions of copies and defined a whole new genre of music, a genre that is still going strong more than 40 years later. Even today, it is a popular opinion that heavy metal is, by its very nature, crap. I don't just mean that some people don't like heavy metal. I mean that a lot of people believe that metal is by its very nature inferior to other sorts of music, and will look down their nose at you for banging your head to Black Sabbath. But what makes music good or bad as art? It just so happens that Black Sabbath's music fulfills some very ancient and respected conceptions about what makes music and lyrics artistically valuable.

Of all the music critics who ever lived, the most influential was the Greek philosopher Aristotle (384–322 BCE). In fact, Aristotle has a pretty good claim to being the most influential person ever in a lot of fields. He wrote ground-breaking works on politics, ethics, logic, metaphysics, biology, and numerous other subjects. It would be difficult to overstate Aristotle's contribution to thought in the Western world. In his *Poetics*, he presents his view of the requirements for

Black Sabbath and Philosophy: Mastering Reality, First Edition. Edited by William Irwin.
© 2013 John Wiley & Sons, Inc. Published 2013 by John Wiley & Sons, Inc.

artistically important comic and tragic verse, including songs. Tragically, we lost Aristotle's work on comedy centuries ago but, funnily enough, his work on tragedy survives. Now, what has this got to do with Black Sabbath?

Far from providing us with grounds to dismiss Black Sabbath's music, Aristotle's account of poetry offers us a framework for the appreciation of Black Sabbath's music as valuable art. Aristotle was born too soon to be a metalhead (by about two and a half thousand years), but given the chance, he just might have found a great deal to like in Black Sabbath. Let's take a closer look at what Aristotle might say about Black Sabbath. To make that easier, let's lift him out of ancient Athens and drop him into Birmingham, England, in 1970, with a burning desire to play in a rock and roll band. He digs the heavier sound being pioneered by bands like Led Zeppelin and Deep Purple, but he's hungry for something with even more edge to it. So he places an ad in a local music shop window—"Aristotle plays full throttle. Needs gig" —and waits for a response.

Bringing Aristotle up to Date

Getting Aristotle to the point where he is ready to audition for Black Sabbath is going to require more than just teaching him English and handing him a guitar. There is a wide gulf in social attitudes between ancient Greek culture and Birmingham youth culture in the late 1960s. Aristotle was a well-bred Greek gentleman. His mother, Phaestis, was of aristocratic descent, and his father, Nicomachus, was personal physician to Amyntas III, king of Macedon. In Greek society, a well-bred gentleman may write poems and songs, but he does *not* play a musical instrument. Aristotle had tremendous respect for music, but in line with the popular attitudes of his day, he despised musicians. In his *Politics*, he writes "we ourselves treat the professors of these arts as mean people, and say that no one would practice them but a drunkard or a buffoon."[1] Aristotle is going to have to lose the attitude if he's going to audition for Black Sabbath, so I'm going to say that he's learned some perspective from living in the twentieth century and has dropped his prejudices against being in a band. Like Lars Ulrich of Metallica and so many other rock musicians, he's going to sweep his middle-class origins far under the rug. When Black Sabbath answer his ad, Aristotle will claim that he was born in Manchester.

The other prejudice that Aristotle will have to lose is his prejudice against artistic innovation. In 1970, Black Sabbath is a wildly experimental group, taking popular music in entirely new directions. Aristotle, on the other hand, is from ancient Greece, where popular entertainment evolves at a slower pace. Some of his specific advice on the topic of music and lyrics seems ridiculously restrictive to us today. When Aristotle describes the categories into which poems and songs have to fit, or discusses the instruments that a musician might use, or even the sort of story-lines that verse should convey, he only has his own cultural tradition to draw on, and his conception of what art can do is necessarily narrow and limited. He doesn't consider the possibility of guitar music, because there *are* no guitars, or the possibility of using a 4/4 beat because nobody had thought of doing that yet.

The limitations on Aristotle's perspective have given him a reputation for being hopelessly artistically conservative—the ultimate square. I don't think that this reputation is fair, though, and I don't think that he is far from being able to accept musical and lyrical innovation. There are two reasons for this.

Firstly, when Aristotle discusses the nature of good music and verse in the *Poetics*, his primary purpose is to describe the state of the art, rather than to tell us the form that good music and verse *must* take. In other words, he is mainly describing good music and verse *as it is* in the fourth century BCE, rather than trying to impose limits on the form. An analogy might be helpful here. Imagine that you are writing a book explaining how to play the electric guitar well. One of the first things you might explain is how to tune a guitar properly. After all, knowing the standard rules for tuning your guitar is important. However, a rule that you must tune your guitar in the standard way can become a limitation on creativity. Black Sabbath *detuned* their guitars in the early 1970s. This detuning produced a distinctive sound that gave Black Sabbath's music a darker quality, and has become a traditional technique in heavy metal music. A rule regarding how guitars must be tuned could prevent this technique. However, when the author of a book on how to play guitars tells you how the strings should be tuned, the author doesn't necessarily mean to say that there can't *possibly* be another legitimate way to tune them. When the author tells you how to play a guitar well, they are just telling you how good guitar playing is currently done, rather than insisting that it is the only possible way to make good guitar music. Similarly, when Aristotle explained in detail how music should be played or how lyrics should be written, his main object was to explain how good art was being produced at the time, rather than to present the only possible ways to produce good music and lyrics.

Secondly, Aristotle understands that a legitimate function of music is simply to provide enjoyment. The mere fact that people like to listen to the music of Black Sabbath makes the music matter as art. He states in *Politics* that music is legitimate even if it does nothing more than bring pleasure and a respite from the stresses and strains of work and life,

> For the end is not desirable for the sake of any future good, nor do the pleasures which we have described exist for the sake of any future good but of the past, that is to say, they are the alleviation of past toils and pains. And we may infer this to be the reason why men seek happiness from these pleasures.[2]

Aristotle even specifically recognizes, in a snotty, condescending way, that music that specifically appeals to the working classes is important simply because the working classes enjoy it. This is so even if it lacks harmony to a more refined ear. He writes:

> [for] the vulgar crowd composed of artisans, laborers, and the like—there ought to be contests and exhibitions instituted for . . . [their] relaxation . . . And the music will correspond to their minds; for as their minds are perverted from the natural state, so there are perverted modes and highly strung and unnaturally colored melodies. A man receives pleasure from what is natural to him, and therefore professional musicians may be allowed to practice this lower sort of music before an audience of the lower type.[3]

So let's allow that Aristotle in 1970 has lost his ancient prejudice against musical innovation. He understands now that radical change can be exactly the sort of shot in the arm that art needs to progress.

Aristotle Joins Black Sabbath

Now Aristotle is almost ready to audition for Black Sabbath. He just needs to get the look right. Diogenes Laertius, who wrote a biography of Aristotle, describes him as an unattractive man with beady eyes and spindly little legs. That's alright; being an ugly bastard never held anyone back in heavy metal. (In what other genre of popular music could Lemmy from Motörhead have a hit, even with a song as good as "Ace of Spades"?) More problematic for Aristotle is that the fashion for men in his day was to have short hair and a full beard. That's not going to look right. Let's have Aristotle grow his hair long like a hippy and shave his beard down to a bushy mustache so that he better fits in with Black Sabbath circa 1970.

What about the gear? Diogenes Laertius tells us that Aristotle "used to indulge in very conspicuous dress, and rings, and used to dress his hair carefully."[4] Perhaps, left to his own devices, Aristotle might opt for a glam-metal look like Mötley Crüe or Poison (or, God help us, KISS). Fortunately, Black Sabbath will stand for none of that. Aristotle will have to settle for a black shirt with a garish silver cross, and occasionally brushing his long hair. Besides, for all his love of conspicuous dress, Aristotle regards it as important that spectacle doesn't detract attention from lyrics and music. Aristotle recognized that it is good to put on a show for the audience, but he believed that producing a spectacle is a less "artistic" achievement than producing music and lyrics—"The spectacle, though an attraction, is the least artistic of all the parts, and has least to do with the art of poetry."[5] When Aristotle finally gets to see theatrical bands like Alice Cooper and Gwar, he will slap his forehead and groan "metal used to be about the *music!*"

What role in Black Sabbath will Aristotle audition for? He probably won't want to play the drums, so Bill Ward is safe there. In Aristotle's culture, drumming was an art mainly pursued by women, so I'm going to guess that being the drummer seems rather effeminate to him. However, he liked to give public lectures, so maybe he would like to be front man in place of Ozzy Osbourne. The band give him a tryout. Unfortunately, Diogenes Laertius tells us that Aristotle spoke with a lisp, so as the philosopher launches into the opening lines of "Black Sabbath," his raw volume and impassioned delivery can't make up for the fact that he's singing "What ith thith that thtandth before me? Figure in black which pointh at me!" Ozzy will remain the lead singer. Aristotle tries out for lead guitar next, but he can't compete with the skill of Tony Iommi. Aristotle suggests that Black Sabbath could employ *two* rhythm guitarists, as Judas Priest do, but Iommi won't budge—Geezer Butler used to a be a rhythm guitarist too, but had to move to bass guitar when he joined. Just to add insult to injury, then, let's have Aristotle join Geezer on the bass.

At least Geezer will still get to write almost all of the lyrics. Or will he? Aristotle wants to have a crack at that too. Aristotle wrote two books of poems and more poetry besides, including a hymn with the verse "For thee what son of Greece would not / Deem it an enviable lot, / To live the life, to die the death / That fears no weary hour, shrinks from no fiery breath?"[6], which are pretty metal lyrics for a hymn. I can imagine Ozzy belting that out on stage. Unfortunately, Aristotle's poems have been lost since ancient times, so let's say that one of Geezer's cigarettes accidentally sets fire to Aristotle's notebook, ending his direct lyrical contribution to Black Sabbath.

What Aristotle does have to offer the band, at the very least, is a capacity to appreciate their work. Stripped from the limitations of specific ancient Greek artistic traditions, Aristotle's conception of what makes for good or bad art offers us a philosophy of art that can recognize and value the importance of what Black Sabbath is doing. As mentioned, Aristotle believes that the pleasure people get from music is justification enough for that music's existence. However, Aristotle has more reason to like Black Sabbath's music than just that he can bang his head to it. In particular, Aristotle in the seventies loves the darkness of Black Sabbath's music, and he loves the band's willingness to reflect on the human condition, even in the form of musical fantasies and nightmares.

The Need for Dark Art

Surely the most controversial aspect of Black Sabbath's music is the sheer darkness it often achieves. With a tone inspired by horror movies, Black Sabbath in the early 1970s often express a sense of negativity and hopelessness that was unprecedented in popular music. Contrary to hysterical folklore, the band never sided with evil and destruction. One of the central messages of their work is that love is better than hate—as exemplified in "Wicked World," "Into the Void," and "A National Acrobat." Another central message found in their albums is that God and the forces of good will win in the end—as exemplified, for instance, in "War Pigs," "After Forever," and "Lord of this World."

Still, the mood evoked by Black Sabbath is often bleak and desperate, as the lyrics explore themes of misery and doom. "Happiness I cannot feel / And love to me is so unreal" wails Ozzy in "Paranoid," turning the hippy lyrical aesthetic of the late 1960s on its head. In "Wheels of Confusion" he complains: "So I found that life is just a game / But you know there's never been a winner / Try your hardest, just to be a loser / The world will still be turning when you're gone." On occasion, things turn dark for the entire world in a Black Sabbath song. Sometimes we face apocalyptic warfare, as in "War Pigs," "Electric Funeral," and "Hole in the Sky." If we are really unlucky, we might even face a rampaging devil as in "Black Sabbath," or worse, an angry God, as in, again, "War Pigs."

Many people find songs with such themes repellant. Why sing about terrible things when you could sing about wonderful things? Why sing about unhappiness and fear when you could sing about positive emotions like joy and security? This is, of course, exactly the sort of sentiment expressed by people who object to horror movies, seeing in them an unhealthy glorification of the negative where there could be an inspiring story of something positive.

Aristotle, however, was a horror junkie, who saw the theater of horror as one of the pinnacles of cultural achievement. Now, when I say that Aristotle was a "horror" junkie, I don't mean that he would recognize the modern film genre that directly influenced Black Sabbath. But he did like plays to be about horrible things happening to people. It was particularly important to him that the characters were sympathetic, that they suffered horribly, and that there was always an unhappy ending. Like other ancient Greeks, he recognized only two types of play: comedies and tragedies. In the surviving book of his *Poetics*, Aristotle discusses good tragedy in detail, and stresses that it is a more important artistic form than both comedy and epic poetry. In case you think I'm cheating by calling Aristotle a "horror junkie," keep in mind that Greek tragedies were hardcore. In Sophocles' play *Oedipus the King*, everyone in the city of Thebes is dying from a plague sent by the gods because of an unsolved murder (the gods didn't *tell* the Thebans that's why they sent a plague; the Thebans were left to work it out). The king of Thebes, Oedipus, is a fine upstanding ruler who always strives to do what is right. He sets out to solve the case, only to learn that he once accidentally killed his own father, and that his wife is really his mother, with whom he has produced several children. Upon learning that her husband is her son, Oedipus' mother commits suicide. Taking all of this about as well as can be expected, King Oedipus rips out his own eyeballs and goes off to live as a wandering homeless lunatic in constant torment. The end.

You would never have been allowed to put a story that horrific in a horror movie in the 1970s, nor will you ever find a tale quite that blackly demented in a Black Sabbath song (in death metal, black metal, or grindcore maybe, but not Sabbath). Aristotle, however, thought that *Oedipus the King* was a really excellent play, about as good a play as he had ever seen. Far from finding the horror and despair repellant or over the top, he believed that the very awfulness of the events depicted was an essential part of what made the play great art.

Aristotle believed that art dealing with negative emotions could purify the soul in accordance with a process that he called *katharsis* (now the word *catharsis* in modern English). Catharsis is the purging of negative emotions, especially fear and pity, by feeling them on behalf of the human subjects of an artistic performance. By feeling fear and pity on behalf of a poor bastard like Oedipus, we get the negative emotions out of our system. In Greek, *katharsis* literally refers to any kind of purging, including the inducement of vomiting. Through exposure to dark art, our soul vomits up the bad emotions, leaving us cleansed.

Aristotle would recognize the cathartic nature of Black Sabbath's music. In their bleakest songs, we are invited to sympathize with people who are suffering. In "Black Sabbath," Ozzy presents himself as every bit as doomed out of nowhere as King Oedipus. A black apparition "with eyes of fire" has suddenly appeared to tell him that, against his will, he is Satan's chosen one ("Oh no!" he says—as you would). Then Satan shows up, everybody is running and screaming, and everything is on fire. It's a good song. Aristotle can perfectly well understand that the very darkness of "Black Sabbath" is an integral element of what makes the song good because it is precisely the horror of the situation that engages our emotions.

Similarly, consider what a noble but abused hero we find in "Iron Man." If we take the lyrics literally, Iron Man has personally saved all of humanity (by traveling in time through a big magnetic field that turned his body to steel, which is bad science even for a metal song). Now nobody wants Iron Man or cares about him. He stands perfectly motionless, but nobody ever tries to help him, though they don't know if he is paralyzed, or even if he is alive or dead. Even if we take the song less literally, perhaps as a metaphor for the treatment of war veterans, the point is that Iron Man has been betrayed and maltreated. Like King Oedipus, he is a highly sympathetic character and an exceptionally unlucky bastard. Like King Oedipus, he engages our sympathies, and through sympathizing with an imaginary person in such a terrible position, we experience catharsis. In apparent acknowledgment of the powers of catharsis, Ozzy concludes "Paranoid" by expressing his hope that hearing about how unhappy he is will make the listener feel better—"And so as you hear these words / Telling you now of my state / I tell you to enjoy life / I wish I could but it's too late."

The Need to Shake up Your Mind

Besides pleasure and catharsis, Aristotle recognized one final function of good art. Good art makes you think. Aristotle claimed that the difference between history and poetry is that "the one describes the thing that has been, and the other a kind of thing that might be. Hence poetry is something more philosophical and of graver import than history."[7] In other words, poetry is more important than history because poetry allows us to imagine alternatives to the way that things have been. It is only by understanding the alternative forms that life can take that we can truly understand our own condition. Black Sabbath explores alternative forms of life not just by channeling extreme personal feelings, but by painting a variety of possible futures for humanity. In "War Pigs," the future holds an apocalyptic war in which evil generals conspire to spread death and hatred, plotting destruction just for fun. In "Electric Funeral," the future holds a quicker, atomic alternative. Instead of burning in the fields as in "War Pigs," we burn at home in a "globe of obscene fire." We brought it on ourselves too, with our own lack of resistance—"Robot minds of robot slaves / Lead them to atomic graves." Presenting yet a third alternative, in "Children of the Grave," the narrator urges the "children of the world" to rise up in the name of love and peace before humanity is destroyed and the "children of today" become "children of the grave." The listener is challenged to think about how good or bad the future may be, and about their own role in our march toward it.

It goes without saying that the songs of Black Sabbath do not present detailed and tightly argued political advice. Aristotle would probably like the band to move further in that direction. He stresses in his book *Rhetoric* that people are best persuaded by well-reasoned arguments. But that isn't what the music of Black Sabbath is for. What we get from Black Sabbath is not a plan for political action, but a dream or nightmare to inspire us to think about our world and our place in it. Aristotle makes it clear in both his *Politics* and his *Nicomachean Ethics* that he is a firm believer in the need for political involvement, on the grounds that the health of our society depends on our being politically active. He states in *Politics* that "If liberty and equality, as is thought by some, are chiefly to be found in democracy, they will be best attained when all persons alike share in the government to the utmost."[8] Now, since Aristotle was writing this in the fourth century BCE, he didn't mean that people like women, or slaves, or non-Greeks should be permitted to vote. All the same, he had cottoned on to the essential idea that healthy government requires everyone to stand up and participate. Given this, Aristotle is able to understand the importance of what Black Sabbath is doing in conjuring fantasies of annihilation and revolution.

Sometimes, of course, Black Sabbath's lyrics take the listener well beyond the realm of probability. Songs like "The Wizard" and "Symptom of the Universe" are pure magical fantasy, while the way that Satan turns up in "Black Sabbath" and God turns up in "War Pigs" owes more to drama than realism. Aristotle is perfectly alright with stretching probability, though. He explicitly tells us that art can legitimately relate wildly improbable events if doing so makes the story better. He says of the poet that "Any impossibilities there may be in his descriptions of things are faults. But from another point of view they are justifiable, if they serve the end of poetry itself—if . . . [that is] they make the effect of either that very portion of the work or some other portion more astounding."[9]

Sweet Leaf?

One last important philosophical question remains to be addressed. Would Aristotle, as a member of Black Sabbath, join in the drinking and drug-taking? You are probably well aware that booze and drugs are an integral part of the story of early Black Sabbath, eventually leading to Ozzy Osbourne's being fired in 1979 for being out of control. When bottles are being opened or joints being passed around, what does Aristotle do? And is he interested in something harder?

Aristotle makes it clear in his *Nicomachean Ethics* that pleasure is an important part of life and that a little bit of self-indulgence is a good thing. He held that drinking, like other physical pleasures, should be pursued in moderation. Over-indulging in alcohol is a bad thing, but Aristotle also thought that it was a character flaw not to be willing to appreciate harmless pleasures like having a drink—"the man who shuns every pleasure, as boors do, becomes in a way insensible."[10] So yes, Aristotle will have a beer, but he won't drink himself into alcoholism. And the sweet leaf? Aristotle will have a puff on that too, thanks. Marijuana was unknown in ancient Greece, but the same principle that recommends drinking in moderation recommends moderate use of weed too. Marijuana is unlike alcohol in that it is illegal, but Aristotle did not believe that all laws are good laws, stating in his *Politics* that "Even when laws have been written down, they ought not always to remain unaltered."[11] Nor did Aristotle believe that a bad law must necessarily be obeyed—when he was wrongfully accused of impiety in Athens, he fled the city rather than obey the law and accept his punishment.

What about harder drugs? As the money starts to roll in, does he turn to cocaine, the bane of early Black Sabbath and the drug that, more than any other, dissolved the original line-up of the band? No, he'll skip the blow, thanks. The same principles of moderation that forbid excessive drinking in *Nicomachean Ethics* forbid the use of cocaine altogether. There is no safe way to dabble moderately in snorting coke. Given how powerful and physically addictive the drug is, any use of it must be considered excessive.

The position on drugs being described is relatively close to that advocated on early Black Sabbath albums, even if the band members themselves didn't always take their own advice. The song "Sweet

Leaf" is a love song to marijuana. The attitude toward it is clear—the sweet leaf is pleasurable, so smoking it is a good thing. Yet Black Sabbath is more eager to warn us about the dangers that lie in drugs than they are to tell us about the pleasures. "Hand of Doom" is an angry harangue against a heroin addict dying from an overdose. "Fairies Wear Boots" could at first be mistaken for psychedelic whimsy, of a sort that other bands had long been doing. But when Pink Floyd or David Bowie saw gnomes, the explanation was magical. When Black Sabbath sees gnomes, the explanation turns out to be much more realistic; there is a drug problem involved. "Snowblind" is a song about the love of cocaine, just as "Sweet Leaf" is a song about the love of marijuana, but here the tone is not joy but impending doom. Ozzy loves the snow, but it is freezing him to death— "Something blowing in my head / Winds of ice that soon will spread / Down to freeze my very soul / Makes me happy, makes me cold."

Ozzy Osbourne did indeed have a serious problem with booze and drugs, including cocaine. He's clean now (good on you Ozzy!), but back in the 1970s things went from bad to worse until he finally split from Black Sabbath in 1979. No doubt Aristotle pleaded with him to show some restraint and moderation, but you cannot reason with somebody who is high. So Ozzy leaves Sabbath and goes on to record *Blizzard of Ozz* (1980) and *Diary of a Madman* (1981). Black Sabbath replace Ozzy on vocals with Ronnie James Dio and go on to record *Heaven and Hell* (1980) and *Mob Rules* (1981). But they do it without Aristotle. The band just doesn't seem the same without Ozzy, and Aristotle follows him out the door. He goes on to write books about ethics, politics, and logic, and to front Iron Maiden, Megadeth, and Äristötlë.

Asked in a 1983 *Rolling Stone* interview to sum up the biggest lesson he learned during his time in Black Sabbath, Aristotle quoted his own *Nicomachean Ethics* ". . . men make themselves responsible for being unjust or self-indulgent, in the one case by cheating and in the other by spending their time in drinking bouts and the like; for it is activities exercised on particular objects that make the corresponding character."[12] What he means by that is

> Black Sabbath was a great band—*is* a great band [*Raises horns*]. We invented heavy metal and we put out a string of classic albums. But if there is one thing I learned in my time with Black Sabbath, it's this: don't risk getting into any habits that you might not easily be able to get yourself out of again.

Notes

1. Aristotle, *Politics, The Complete Works of Aristotle*, ed. J. Barnes (Princeton: Princeton University Press, 1984), Book VIII, 2125.
2. Ibid., Book VIII, 2125.
3. Ibid., Book VIII, 2129.
4. Diogenes Laertius, *The Lives and Opinions of Eminent Philosophers*, trans. R.D. Hicks (Cambridge, MA: Harvard University Press, 1925), Book XI, 181.
5. Aristotle, Poetics, *The Complete Works of Aristotle*, ed. J. Barnes (Princeton: Princeton University Press, 1984), 2321.
6. Diogenes Laertius, *The Lives and Opinions of Eminent Philosophers*, Book XI, 183.
7. Aristotle, *Poetics*, 2323.
8. Aristotle, *Politics*, Book IV, 2050.
9. Aristotle, *Poetics*, 2337.
10. Aristotle, *Nicomachean Ethics, The Complete Works of Aristotle*, ed. J. Barnes (Princeton: Princeton University Press, 1984), Book II, 1744.
11. Aristotle, *Politics*, Book II, 2014.
12. Aristotle, *Nicomachean Ethics*, Book III, 1758–1759.

Chapter 8

Black Sabbath and the Problem of Defining Metal

Søren R. Frimodt-Møller

Determining what bands count and what bands don't count as metal is a perennial subject of debate and discussion among metal fans. The answers each fan gives depend largely on the criteria they establish for what heavy metal is. In this chapter, I offer a slightly different approach to the issue. I argue that a particular kind of connection to Black Sabbath is what qualifies a band as metal. A true metal band must be either inspired by Black Sabbath or be inspired by other bands that are inspired by Black Sabbath.

So, is there a specific degree of Black Sabbath influence that qualifies a band as metal? Well, not quite. There are a lot of other factors that affect whether a band is accepted as being metal, some of which depend on the historical context of the music. For instance, consider stoner rock, a genre in which the ideal seems to be to sound like Black Sabbath on *Master of Reality*. Back in the seventies, this music would have been called heavy metal, but today it falls within the realm of rock, pure and simple. The standards of what qualifies as metal are constantly changing.

With respect to "noisiness," a lot of what was considered noisy in the seventies sounds quite settled and radio-friendly in comparison with the thrash metal bands of the 1980s, which again are not as distorted and sonically overwhelming as many extreme metal bands from the 1990s and 2000s.

A different trait, the use of down-tuned guitars and basses, has also developed over the years. On the early Black Sabbath albums, Tony

Black Sabbath and Philosophy: Mastering Reality, First Edition. Edited by William Irwin.
© 2013 John Wiley & Sons, Inc. Published 2013 by John Wiley & Sons, Inc.

Iommi and Geezer Butler pioneered these alternative tunings, which sounded dark and ominous at the time.[1] As a contrast, consider the album *Pineappleskunk*, issued in 2001 by Doug Pinnick from the rock band King's X under the moniker Poundhound. *Pineappleskunk* features guitar and bass that are tuned down to such an extent that the actual pitches are often barely distinguishable.[2] The album is a bit of a borderline case, but listening to it today, I think the music is structurally closer to rock music, pure and simple, in the tradition of Jimi Hendrix, than it is to heavy metal.

Although there is a general emphasis on rhythm structures in metal, the palette of rhythms that are allowed in metal today is so varied that it is difficult to draw sharp boundaries between this palette and, say, today's arsenal of rhythms used in much electronic music (techno, trip hop, drum 'n' bass, and others).

So the bottom line is that I do not think we can specify exact stylistic traits that one has to follow in order to be a metal artist. I do, however, think that for a given heavy metal artist or band, we can trace the reason why the artist is accepted as metal back through the chain of relationships between their music and the music of Black Sabbath. Before I offer some cases in support of this hypothesis, let's first consider a different, but related question: Why do we need categories?

Why Do We Need Categories?

Many rock and metal musicians hate being categorized. They think being identified with a specific genre impedes their freedom of musical expression. If fans come to expect a certain type of music from a band, the band risks upsetting the fans if they choose a new stylistic direction. (This is a justified fear, considering the controversies in connection with the release of Metallica's *Load* or, more recently, Opeth's *Heritage*, Morbid Angel's *Illud Divinus Insanus*, and The Haunted's *Unseen*—and indeed in connection with several Black Sabbath releases, especially after the departure of Ozzy in 1979.) So why do we need to lump artists into genre categories?

The short answer is that music consumers need genres because they like going back to music that does certain things for them, or has certain typical traits. A genre is a category that helps us identify something.

There may be a lot of different hammers of different sizes, shapes, colors, and materials, but if I say "I need a hammer," I just want you to help me find one of these objects that will let me bang a nail into a wall. I would think you were a raving lunatic if you brought me a fish bowl instead. Similarly, if I am browsing in the metal section in a CD store, I expect that there will be a lot of varied music in that section, some of which I will not like, but I do not expect to find Sting or Steely Dan albums stored alongside Slayer and Strapping Young Lad.

The concept of genre can be traced back to Aristotle (384–322 BC), who liked to divide everything in the world (this is not really an exaggeration) into categories, families, sub-concepts, and so on. For any specific substance, he wanted to know if it belonged to the same "genus" as other substances, the same overarching concept. Later in world history, Austrian-Hungarian monk and botanist Gregor Mendel (1822–1884) derived the word "gene" from "genus," because he was advocating the existence of certain entities in organisms that they inherit from their family, and which determine the kind of things the organism can be. But enough etymology.

Metal Conditions?

Defining a genre can be very difficult, but to facilitate the process philosophers often speak of *necessary* and *sufficient* conditions. A necessary condition for being x is something that a thing needs in order to be x. That does not mean that you are automatically an x, if you fulfill the necessary condition. But if you do not fulfill the condition, you are certainly not an x. So, for example, having four sides is a necessary condition for being a square. Anything that is a square must have four sides. But there are some geometrical figures that have four sides but are not squares, such as trapezoids. A sufficient condition for being x, is something that, if a thing fulfills it, makes us sure that the thing is indeed an x. If we can provide conditions for being x that are both necessary *and* sufficient, then we have a precise definition of x. So, for example, having four equal sides and four equal angles are each necessary conditions for being a square. In this case when a figure has both necessary conditions—four equal sides *and* four equal angles—this is sufficient for being a square.

While it's easy and uncontroversial to list the necessary and sufficient conditions for being a square, it's not at all easy or uncontroversial to list the necessary and sufficient conditions for being a metal band. Sufficient conditions for metal might include the combination of energetic double pedaling on the bass drums, growling vocals, or tuned-down guitars and bass. None of these traits, however, is a necessary condition. Why not? Because it is possible to be a metal band and not have any of these traits. For instance, it is not until 1990's *TYR* that double pedaling is heard on a Black Sabbath album.[3] There is a similar use of figures on the toms in "Children of the Grave" from *Master of Reality*, and Sabbath introduced fast, thrash-like tempos on the *Paranoid* album. But just to end the discussion of whether fast tempos and double-pedaling is a necessary condition for being heavy metal, think of the self-titled opening track from the first Black Sabbath album, "Black Sabbath." The song is heavy in the intuitive sense of the word—it is very slow, and sounds like the soundtrack to someone dragging a very heavy object across the ground. "Black Sabbath" is arguably the world's first doom metal song. In fact, the subgenre of doom metal is one of the few metal subgenres that actually *has* at least one necessary condition, namely ultra-slow tempos. Of course, there can be doom metal with a lot of double-pedaling on top of the basic tempo, but still, you pretty much have time to run out and get a beer within each bar.

Tuned-down guitars could, arguably, be a necessary condition within a given historical time, but standards have changed with respect to how much something can be tuned down in the first place and still remain within the realm of plain rock music. So even if alternate tuning is a necessary condition for metal, it is too broad to help us say anything about what metal is in opposition to other genres. Alternate tuning is not a sufficient condition for metal; it is not enough. The same goes for the use of distortion. And if you seriously think that all metal bands use growls, then why are you reading this book?

So, at least if we are talking about heavy metal as a whole, and not about more specific subgenres, it seems that we cannot give a definition in the sense of one or more conditions that are both necessary and sufficient.

All in the Sabbath Family

In music reviews we often read statements like this: "These San Francisco newcomers play a heavy, yet melodic bay area thrash in the tradition of Forbidden." Personally, when I write a review of an album (which I do now and then), the attribution of a certain genre or sub-genre label is a point I reach after having associated the music with some specific bands I already know. For instance I may think, "This sounds a bit like early Dream Theater, it has a bit of inspiration from Symphony X from the post-*V* era, and even some vocals that sound inspired by Daniel Gildenlöw from Pain of Salvation," and then begin my review with "this band plays progressive metal in the tradition of Dream Theater and Symphony X, but with a bit of the darker twist of modern progressive rock bands like Pain of Salvation." As you can tell, progressive metal is one of my favorite subgenres, but occasionally I have been assigned to review a band in a genre I knew nothing about in advance, for instance black metal. In the case of the black metal album review, I called up a friend and asked him if he could give me a crash course in the genre. Can you guess what the first thing he did was? Right, he gave me a list of influential artists that characterize what is known as black metal.

Actual cases of the use of a concept have always been one of the best ways to learn to use the concept in question. This is a key part of the language theory developed by Austrian philosopher Ludwig Wittgenstein (1889–1951) in the later part of his life. Wittgenstein not only held that we learn the meaning of a word by using it in specific situations, he also held that the *only* way to understand the meaning of a word is by taking part in a situation where it makes sense to use the word. As with many theories of language, Wittgenstein's philosophy is difficult to defend, if we take it universally. If we think of music, however, the idea makes a lot of sense. It is, in fact, quite difficult, if not impossible to teach people the difference between "major" and "minor" chords, without actually playing the chords for them (even if very exact definitions of the structural differences between these harmonies exist). Likewise, it is impossible for me to give a meaningful description of what makes the first three Black Sabbath albums so different from any other music that came before 1970, without assuming that you have actually heard some of these records. I could write that the albums broke new ground by being riff-oriented in a way that not even Jimi Hendrix had conceived of, with Ozzy's vocals and the rhythmical figures of both bass and drums accenting the structure of the guitar riff (think of songs like "N.I.B.," "Iron Man," and "Into the Void"), that the bass and drum parts quickly became as important as the guitar parts (something that is a typical trait of heavy metal, even though it is not a necessary condition), that they pioneered down-tuned guitar and bass, and so on. But none of this would make any sense to you, if you did not have a sonic reference—in other words, the actual recordings—to listen to.

Wittgenstein further had the idea that the specific cases in which we use some words and concepts relate to each other like a family. Think of the way family resemblance works. I'll bet that in your own family you will not be able to find one single trait that *everyone* in your family shares, apart from the general traits you share with all human beings or with other members of a particular ethnicity. Yet, some people in your family may be a little like someone else in your family, who in turn have traits similar to other people, and so on, thus forming a family resemblance. Wittgenstein held that some words and concepts work this way, "game" for example. According to Wittgenstein, there is nothing that all games have in common. That is, there are no necessary or sufficient conditions for being a game.[4] Instead, what we call games share an overlapping network of characteristics; they share a family resemblance. Wittgenstein would probably have considered "heavy metal" a family resemblance concept in the same way as "game." There are no necessary and sufficient conditions for being metal. Instead, bands we call metal share an overlapping network of characteristics. And in this case the family begins with Black Sabbath.

Black Sabbath as a Prototype for Heavy Metal

So how do you start a new family? According to *prototype theories*, a concept is defined in relation to a prototype, a basic or original instance. There can be varying degrees of resemblance, so sometimes it can be debatable whether the concept applies to a case or not. For example, when we talk about a chair, we normally have a definition in terms of the function of the object, namely that it is something we can sit on. There are, however, a lot of objects we can sit on that are not chairs, like couches, low tables, and large rocks. When we think of a chair, pure and simple, we have an idea of a very typical object with four legs, a rest for your back, and so on. And it is by resemblance with this "prototype" that we categorize other objects as chairs. Some objects will inarguably be called chairs, even if they don't have four legs, whereas other objects will invite some discussion as to whether we can really call them chairs (is a "Fatboy" a chair?). This is slightly different from Wittgenstein's theory, because we actually have one set of traits that everything else belonging to the concept resembles. We still have to know other members of the "family," though, because we need to learn how much and in which ways cases can differ from the prototype.

I would argue that all musical genres have prototypes, and that Black Sabbath is the first, and one of the most important prototypes of heavy metal. It is impossible to say exactly what features a band must have in common with Black Sabbath in order to be called metal, but it is safe to say that every heavy metal band has some tie to Black Sabbath's music—if not by direct inspiration, then at least by inspiration from other bands that are directly inspired by Black Sabbath.

As previously mentioned, doom metal has its roots in the song "Black Sabbath" and slow tempos on songs such as "War Pigs," "Keep It Warm," and "After All (The Dead)," just to choose some examples from different eras.

Thrash as we know it today would not be what it is without eighties thrash metal artists such as Metallica and Slayer, but the raw, blunt, and fast energy of the genre can be traced back to Sabbath songs such as "Paranoid" and "Symptom of the Universe." The latter even has the same dark, alternately minor-scale and disharmonic chord pattern of much later thrash metal (if we ignore the quiet, Doors-like section that ends the piece). Try comparing the rhythm structure of the Metallica song "Master of Puppets" with that of "Paranoid," or try comparing one of Slayer's slower songs with "Symptom of the Universe" and you'll hear what I mean.

Death metal is, of course, dependent on the use of growls. But you can still draw clear lines from the type of unison band riffs (where guitar, bass, drums, and vocals follow each other) in death metal to Black Sabbath's performances on *Paranoid* and *Master of Reality*. One could also argue that the dark, ominous atmosphere of not only death metal, but also gothic metal, black metal, and, again, doom, all began in the music of Black Sabbath.

Progressive metal has championed the use of long, eclectic songs with lots of contrasts between soft, melodic passages, incorporation of different styles of music, and heavy sections. On their first album Black Sabbath played with such eclectic structures in "Wicked World," and they took these experiments to new levels on songs like "Under the Sun/Every Day Comes and Goes" from *Vol. 4*, "Killing Yourself to Live"[5] and the title track from *Sabbath Bloody Sabbath*, "Dirty Women" from *Technical Ecstasy*, and "Air Dance" from *Never Say Die!* just to name a few.

Power metal may in general have Iron Maiden as its main prototype, but actually the first two releases from Black Sabbath's Dio-era, *Heaven and Hell* and *Mob Rules*, were an influence on Iron Maiden, and remain important references for today's power metal bands. Iron Maiden's Bruce Dickinson has acknowledged that "Children of the Sea" from *Heaven and Hell* was an inspiration for "Children of the Damned," and there are similarities between the main riffs of "Country Girl" from *Mob Rules* and the Maiden song "To Tame a Land."

Born Again was panned by a lot of fans and critics at the time, but actually the album was genuinely inventive. "Zero the Hero" was an influence on Guns N' Roses (who claim the song was an inspiration for "Paradise City"), and the track's steadily pulsing, hypnotic groove sounds like an ancestor of later acts such as Tool and OSI. "Disturbing the Priest" from *Born Again* is a very clear source of inspiration for the later psychedelic progressive metal pioneers Psychotic Waltz. Even the vocals on "Disturbing the Priest" sound like something straight off the first two Psychotic Waltz albums. Adding to the evidence, Psychotic Waltz actually recorded a cover of "Disturbing the Priest" for a special edition of their 1993 album *Into the Everflow*.

It's not clear if any grunge should count as metal, but two of the most metal-sounding grunge bands, Soundgarden and Alice in Chains, have clear connections to Black Sabbath. Soundgarden were much inspired by the sound on *Master of Reality*; they even did a cover of "Into the Void" for the EP *Satanoscillatemymetallicsonatas*. If you listen to Alice in Chains with *Sabotage* in mind, you get the feeling that this album is part of their heritage, in particular the eerie vocal harmonies on "Megalomania" and "Am I Going Insane (Radio)." Actually, the groove of some heavier parts of *Sabotage*, such as

"Hole in the Sky," also foreshadows the first Alice in Chains album, *Facelift*.

Let's not forget *Dehumanizer*, Sabbath's sort-of comeback album from 1992 (reuniting the *Mob Rules* line-up after several years with Tony Iommi as the only original member). The album is a reference for some of the bands that emerged in the mid-1990s, especially Nevermore and Symphony X. Both bands combine power metal and thrash with theatrical atmospheres, raw high-register vocals, and progressive technical prowess (although with very different outcomes), all prominent features on *Dehumanizer*. The media critique running through songs like "Computer God" and "TV Crimes" also sounds like an inspiration for the lyrics on Nevermore's "Poison God Machine," and Symphony X even have a song called "Dehumanized" on their *Iconoclast* album.

As is well known, Black Sabbath introduced the use of occult and satanic themes to the lyrics and imagery of metal. In preparation for a lecture in which I discussed certain types of album covers, I realized that the reason why a particular cover, the one for the album *Behind the Black Veil* by The Shadow Theory, still looked like a heavy metal cover, even though it just pictured a slightly spooky-looking old house in twilight with a ghostlike figure in front of it, was that it conjured the imagery of the first Black Sabbath album cover. Other influential metal images from Sabbath include the demons on the cover of *Sabbath Bloody Sabbath* and the weirdly malfunctioning mirror on the cover of *Sabotage*. And last but not least, it was Ronnie James Dio who popularized the classic metal horns gesture at Black Sabbath's concerts in the early 1980s.

Of course, there are some problems with letting the connection to Black Sabbath's music define an artist as belonging within the realm of heavy metal. For example, even though "The Wizard" sounds like something Queens of the Stone Age could have written today, that hardly makes Queens of the Stone Age a metal band. As we've noted, standards change concerning how aggressive, noisy, and down-tuned music can be without being called metal.

There is also the question of who came first, when we try to determine the influence of Black Sabbath. Even though you can hear similarities between the Sabbath releases with Tony Martin on vocals and metal bands that were in vogue at the time these albums came out, that does not make Black Sabbath an influence on these bands in virtue of these releases alone. For example, it wouldn't make any sense to say that "Virtual Death" from Sabbath's *Cross Purposes* (1994) was an influence on Alice in Chains' "Junkhead" from their album *Dirt* (1992). It is also highly unlikely that Black Sabbath had an influence on, say, Rage Against the Machine via the song "Illusion of Power," which featured a rap by Ice-T, since the album *Forbidden* that included the song came out in 1995, more than two years after Rage Against the Machine's debut album.

Go Forth and Find New Prototypes

In today's metal community, Black Sabbath have been, if not replaced by, then supplemented with, other prototypes, but these prototypes themselves all have important direct or indirect connections to Black Sabbath. No matter which subgenre we consider, we have the same problems when trying to define the genre, as we have with defining, say, heavy metal in general: There will always be certain members of a genre that are located there dependent on historical factors (the standards at a given time), and members that we are not quite sure belong there (borderline cases that are very far from the prototypes of the genre). Still, it makes sense to use genre concepts because there will always be artists and bands that inarguably belong within a specific genre, and just as importantly, artists that certainly do *not* belong in the given category.

So let the debates continue. And may you enjoy refining the definitions of heavy metal for years to come!

Notes

1. At least from *Master of Reality* and onward. The use of drop-tunings on the first two albums is debated. Martin Popoff says that the down-tuning started on *Master of Reality*. See his *Black Sabbath: Doom Let Loose* (Toronto: ECW Press, 2006), 57; Paul Wilkinson says that "Warning" from the debut album was the first song with down-tuning. See his *Rat Salad: Black Sabbath The Classic Years 1969–1975* (New York: Thomas Dunne Books, 2006), 51.
2. The songs "Somedays" and "Jumpin" are representative examples.

3. If double-pedaling is used on previous Black Sabbath albums, it is done very subtly.
4. This is a point of discussion. One could argue that all games fulfill the necessary condition of involving certain rules that you have to follow in order to play the game, whether you are playing chess or playing with dolls.
5. The track is actually a suite including two other short songs, "You Think that I'm Crazy" and "I Don't Know If I'm Up or Down."

Chapter 9

Saint Vitus Dance
The Art of Doom

Manuel Bremer and Daniel Cohnitz

If you saw someone suffering from Sydenham's Chorea, you might not realize that the person has a disease. In fact, with all the jerking and rapid movements, you might think the person was dancing. They don't call it Saint Vitus Dance for nothing. You might even think the dance was pretty good. Of course, from the subjective perspective of the infected person there is nothing artistic or beautiful about it. The movements are not intended as dance in the first place. It is not art.

Unlike people suffering from St Vitus Dance, artists usually intend their products to be works of art. But artistic intention alone isn't enough. So what makes something a work of art? In particular, what makes a song like "St. Vitus Dance" a work of art? As we'll see, the most promising theory of art identifies artworks by placing them in a story that connects them with the history of art. And it is just this kind of story that validates Sabbath's sound of doom as art.

The Devil's Dictionary

Philosophers have forever struggled to define art, but if we believe the *Devil's Dictionary*, such attempts are doomed from the start. There it says:

Art, *n.* This word has no definition.[1]

Black Sabbath and Philosophy: Mastering Reality, First Edition. Edited by William Irwin.
© 2013 John Wiley & Sons, Inc. Published 2013 by John Wiley & Sons, Inc.

And indeed, the history of philosophical attempts to define art is a long story of failures.[2] Most definitions of art attempt to find one characteristic that all and only artworks share. Art, however, exists in such an overwhelming variety of forms that there is no single characteristic that is abstract and general enough, such that all artworks share that characteristic and such that it is really only artworks that have that characteristic in common. Just consider a sculpture by Michelangelo on the one hand and Sabbath's "St. Vitus Dance" on the other. Or consider the cover artwork by Drew Struzan on *Sabbath Bloody Sabbath* and Pyotr Ilyich Tchaikovsky's opera *Eugene Onegin*. What do all of these have in common? There is no clear answer.

What About Paint Vomited onto a Canvas?

Plato (428–348 BCE) thought that the point of good works of art is to imitate aspects of the world as closely and realistically as possible. Sculptures should realistically resemble the shape of human beings, paintings should closely resemble the looks of the landscape or scene they represent, and music should resemble the sound of the human voice—so much for Ozzy. While Plato's imitation requirement makes sense in some periods in the history of art (the Renaissance, for example), it is not a feature that all works of art have in common. Just think about the cover-art on *Technical Ecstasy* by Hipgnosis, which is meant to represent two robots screwing on an escalator, but which doesn't realistically imitate anything in the actual world.

This point is even more obvious if you think about non-representational art, like paintings by Jackson Pollock, which look as if somebody vomited paint onto a canvas. Pollock's paintings don't imitate or represent anything, not even vomited paint on canvas. In order to deal with non-imitative and non-representational art, philosophers tried to define art in terms of expression. The idea that expressive properties make something art seems on track if you think about metal. "War Pigs," for example, expresses anger about war and the fact that rich people and politicians initiate wars that cost the lives of poor people. Along these lines, Leo Tolstoy (1828–1910) defended a theory of art that defines art as essentially expressing emotions. The idea that artworks essentially express emotions has several problems, however. First, it is not clear what it means for a piece of art, like a song or a painting, to express emotions. Paintings, for example, are inanimate objects. They don't have mental states and thus don't have emotions. People have emotions, but what would it mean to say that, for example, "Snowblind" expresses confusion? Many people (especially fans of boring and overrated blues musicians like Eric Clapton) seem to believe that authenticity requires the musician to go through deep emotions when playing a song. In fact, though, few artists feel the emotions that their artworks express in the moment of creation or performance. Obviously, most paintings and novels take weeks or months or years to complete, and their creators certainly have more than one emotion during this process.

Likewise, an artwork doesn't have to cause the audience to feel the emotion it expresses. A song like "Wicked World" that expresses the pain and frustration caused by some injustice, for example, might actually cause anger in the audience rather than pain and frustration. Thus artworks express emotions only in a metaphorical way.[3] Beyond that, a lot of contemporary conceptual art does not express anything at all.

Coughing Art

Because naturally occurring phenomena, like a case of Saint Vitus Dance and a pretty sunset, are not art, it seems that artworks must be intentionally manufactured by someone who wants to produce an artwork. The development of modern art, however, showed that even this minimal requirement for art doesn't hold. Consider Marcel Duchamp's *Fountain*, which is just a standard Bedfordshire model urinal from the J.L. Mott Iron Works. Or think of Tony Iommi's involuntary cough that was recorded and used as the beginning of "Sweet Leaf." Such "found art" has led to the idea that to qualify as an artwork all that is required is that someone acting on behalf of "the artworld" confers the status of an artwork. Since you and I don't belong to the artworld (assuming we aren't artists, or collectors, curators, or critics), we can't turn non-art into art. Artists and critics can do so, however, provided that the rest of the artworld accepts their proposal. Thus, Sabbath's sound of doom is art, because the artworld—critics and historians of rock—have agreed to accept it as art.

Although this institutional theory highlights the fact that art is a complex business backed by a complex social institution ("the artworld" and the music industry), it doesn't explain why any particular object actually is art. The theory just says that it is art, because it is treated as art by the artworld. This gets us nowhere in terms of understanding of what art is and how it works.

A better account is provided by the historical definition of art, as developed by the contemporary philosopher Jerrold Levinson. The historical definition requires that to count as an artwork, an object must be intended to be regarded-as-a-work-of-art in a way that objects already considered works of art are regarded. So artworks are phenomena (objects, performances, and so on) that can be placed in a narrative that connects them with the rest of the history of art. This is precisely what we would normally do if, say, someone challenged the art status of Duchamp's *Fountain*, or Pollock's drippings. We would tell a story that explains how these pieces were reactions to what was going on in the history of art at their time, and how these objects should be seen as an interesting and important contribution to the progress of art.

Was Doom in the Air?

We love Sabbath now; the music has aged well and influenced countless metal musicians. But we really wish we could have seen Sabbath in 1969 or 1970. They were utterly unique at the time. As James Hetfield of Metallica says, "Sabbath was everything that the 60s weren't. Their music was so cool because it was completely anti-hippie."[4] But if something is too unique we won't be able to place it in the story of art. We won't be able to connect it with what comes before and after. So what led to Sabbath's sound? Was doom in the air?

To get a sense of what occurs with innovation, let's compare the appearance of a new musical style to the discovery of a new scientific theory. Was relativity theory in the air in 1905/1915? Science makes a lot fuss about its pop stars like Einstein, but Einstein's theories did not come out of the blue. He tried to solve problems of the physical theories of his day. Special Relativity was proposed as a breakthrough solution to some of these problems (like inertia). After Einstein published the Special Theory of Relativity, the German mathematician

David Hilbert came up with General Relativity even before Einstein did (in 1915). The moves from Special to General Relativity were what we might call "forced moves."[5]

If the arguments for a new theory are compelling, the scientific community is forced to accept the theory's superiority to its predecessors. Einstein's ingenuity helped to come up with Special Relativity, but it is a safe bet that if Einstein had not come up with it in 1905 somebody else would have come up with it some time later. In fact, there are plenty of examples of two or more scientists working independently of each other and coming up with (more or less) the same theory. A paradigm example of this is the invention of computability theory and the advance of early computers. So, scientific discoveries involve ingenuity, but they also involve logical and theoretical constraints. They are forced moves. One can, with some effort, reconstruct them once one has understood their predecessor theories or problems. What this means is that if you have the choice to save a piece of art (say the original painting of the *Heaven and Hell* album cover, which Geezer Butler tried to buy for his living room) or a new paper by an eminent scientist, you should save the piece of art. The artwork is unique and cannot be easily replaced. The paper by the scientist, if it has real scientific quality, can be rewritten by him or somebody else (some time).[6]

Back to music—was Sabbath's sound of doom a forced move? Certainly not. That is one of the great differences between science and art. We can often construct an artistic genealogy, but not in the explanatory and logical fashion we can in the history of science. Artistic creativity can be far more unique than scientific creativity. Those four guys from Birmingham—the real Fab Four—came up with something nobody had in his books or her inner ear.

On the other hand, even artistic creativity takes place in an "artistic landscape" or "artistic space." The further away some location is, the more creative force is needed to leap forward to it. So, for example, given the musical equipment of the sixties, early black metal, like Venom, was technically feasible, but it was way too far off in artistic space to appear then. It needed stepping stones to get there, the most important of which was the music of Black Sabbath. So Venom may have a cool sound and shocking image, but they were not a huge leap forward from Sabbath and other metal bands of the seventies. In fact, Venom was a pretty predictable development. To take another example, Metallica has some claim to being a major development in metal, but even they were not as innovative as Sabbath. Thanks to Motörhead, Venom, and the new wave of British heavy metal, the ingredients for thrash were in the air when Metallica came on the scene. If Metallica had not pioneered thrash, then Anthrax or Exodus would have led the way. Likewise, it was just a small and natural step from Slayer to the death metal of Morbid Angel.[7]

But there was nothing close to Black Sabbath in 1968 when they first got together. Some pieces of Iron Butterfly have a similar slow speed and down-tuned sound, but the crucial role of keyboards in Iron Butterfly leads at best to something like the early Uriah Heep, who are heavy, but far off from Sabbath's sound of doom. So doom in 1968 was able to find a place in the artistic landscape of rock music, but it wasn't in the air like blues rock.

In contrast, consider Sabbath's peers and rivals. Deep Purple, for example, started as a beat rock band, and when they evolved with *Deep Purple in Rock* in 1970 their anthems (like "Speed King" and "Black Night") took up the style of stomping rock 'n roll, with a lot of added keyboards. Deep Purple were great, but they were also a predictable development of earlier blues rock. Combining elements of folk and blues rock, Led Zeppelin created something new, but it wasn't impossible to see them coming. Unlike Purple and Zeppelin, however, Sabbath was an unpredictable creative breakthrough.

Standards of Doom

Whether you like an artwork or not is up to your subjective taste. Arguments in science can—or should—force a rational audience to agree on a conclusion or come up with stronger counter-arguments. But argumentation plays a different role with art. In arguing that the *Sabbath Bloody Sabbath* cover painting is sublime and that title track is magnificent, you don't try to leave your audience no option but to agree. Rather, you try to make your audience understand, to see why you appreciate this art. You outline what makes it outstanding for you. All this has a subjective dimension, as you stress your perspective and understanding or appreciation of the art. But it also has an objective dimension. The features you direct the audience's attention to (whether they are in the piece of art itself or whether they concern its relation to its cultural environment and tradition) can be understood and evaluated by your audience independently of their agreement with your subjective taste. So subjective discourse on art appeals to the objective features of a piece of art.

An artistic style is generally defined by its structural features, the presence and development of which in an individual piece of art allows us to debate and determine whether it is a successful example of its genre or not. Often, a style can be better understood over time. The musical label "doom" did not exist in 1969; even "heavy metal" didn't come into the musical lexicon until the early seventies. With hindsight and the further development of that subgenre in the eighties, though, we see more clearly (more objectively) now what distinguishes doom from other subgenres of metal or hard rock.

Black Sabbath is the paradigm doom band. Doom is a version of rock music defined, in part, by its down-tuned guitar sound, the dominance of slow guitar riffs, longer song structures, and gloomy lyrics. Some features of doom are shared with other subgenres (like gloomy lyrics in black metal and death metal). Some very general features (like having an electric bass player going with the melody line) can take on a life of their own by the way an individual (like Geezer Butler) brings them to life. And some features are negative only (like the absence or subordinate role of keyboards in traditional doom). With these musical features, Black Sabbath established the standard by which we can judge if other music counts as doom.

That doom has objective features does not mean that the members of Black Sabbath planned them. If their biographies can be trusted, they did not plan much of anything. Geezer Butler's lyrics and the band's name sprang from his fascination with horror movies and the dark side. The sometimes howling sound of the vocals just came from Ozzy Osbourne's voice and vocal range. Tony Iommi used lighter strings on his guitar, after he had cut off his finger tips by accident, and tuned down his guitar additionally to reduce string tension. That contributed to the lower sound of his guitar and their songs in general, especially because Geezer Butler followed Iommi's practice and also tuned his bass three half-steps down. But, as Tony Iommi stresses in the introduction of his autobiography, attributing the invention of doom (or heavy metal) to these accidents would be overstating the case. After all, his hearing was not damaged in the accident. Sabbath was influenced by the Beatles and the blues rock of the time, and they fit in the rock tradition of their time. It's just that they took things in a direction that no one could have anticipated.

Thus the objective features of a style (doom in this case) establish themselves at least in part behind the back of the practitioners. A style develops a life of its own.

Sons of Sabbath

The objectivity of an artistic standard shows itself in the ways it can be adapted and developed. For example, prominent features can be exaggerated and taken to their extremes.

Apart from (traditional) doom following the style of the original Black Sabbath in bands like Saint Vitus, Electric Wizard,[8] and Count Raven, new sub-genres have developed, one of which is drone, a subgenre of doom most associated with the bands Sunn O))) and Earth (and several mixed line-up releases from the record label Southern Lord). Karma To Burn arrived at a somewhat similar style from the direction of stoner rock. Drone—especially Earth, whose leader Dylan Carson seems to have coined the very term "drone" —is mostly instrumental music, slow, focussed on individual riffs and tones, often lacking themes in the usual sense.

Isolating and perfecting elements of drone, *Sunn O)))* takes to the extreme what Black Sabbath invented with doom in pieces like "Electric Funeral" and "Under the Sun/Every Day Comes and Goes." So not only did Sabbath set the stage for future developments in heavy metal in general, but they specifically set the standard for doom, which was then refined into drone.

Though Sabbath's appearance on the scene was unpredictable, some of the ways in which their sound has been developed by others are not surprising. Despite their tremendous influence and the degree to which they have been imitated, Sabbath still sounds remarkably fresh. As Dave Wynhof of Monster Magnet says, "When I was a kid Black Sabbath was the future. Melody, doom and groove proved a potent combination and a highly original one. Nothing has changed. No one has rivalled. When I was a kid, Black Sabbath was the future . . . they still are."[9] We agree.

Notes

1. Ambrose Bierce, *The Devil's Dictionary* (1911), www.thedevilsdictionary. com/?A.
2. Which, again, is something that the *Devil's Dictionary* would have predicted, since it defines *philosophy* as "A route of many roads leading from nowhere to nothing," www.thedevilsdictionary.com/?P. We hope to show in this chapter that this definition is not quite fair.
3. See Nelson Goodman, *Languages of Art* (Indianapolis: Hackett, 2nd ed., 1976).
4. Quoted from the booklet accompanying the CD *Nativity in Black: A Tribute to Black Sabbath*.
5. Daniel Dennett, *Darwin's Dangerous Idea* (London: Penguin, 1996), 128–129.
6. This example is adapted from Nicholas Humphrey, "Scientific Shakespeare," *The Guardian*, August 26, 1987.
7. We owe the last observations to William Irwin.
8. The names of some of these bands are telling if you know the titles of Black Sabbath songs: Saint Vitus (Dance), Iron Man, (Behind the) Walls of Sleep, (Electric) Wizard ....
9. Quoted from the booklet accompanying the CD *Nativity in Black II: A Tribute to Black Sabbath*.

Chapter 10

Gods, Drugs, and Ghosts
Finding Dionysus and Apollo in Black Sabbath and the Birth of Heavy Metal

Dennis Knepp

The gods Dionysus and Apollo were there at the birth of heavy metal. They watched Ozzy Osbourne post "OZZY ZIG NEEDS GIG Experienced front man, owns own PA system." Through a Django Reinhardt album, the gods inspired Tony Iommi to keep playing guitar after he lost two fingertips. When Geezer Butler painted his apartment matte black with numerous inverted crosses and pictures of Satan, it was Apollo who frightened Geezer during his sleep. Dionysus taught Bill Ward to smoke banana peels.

Dionysus and Apollo are pre-Christian pagan gods from ancient Greece. Christians turned the old gods into demons and devils—Christians made them evil. But the old gods were not evil; they were before good and evil in the Christian sense. Black Sabbath has been accused of being evil and Satanic since its first album; but it was never evil or Satanic. Black Sabbath draws upon gods that are older than Satan. Black Sabbath is both primal and electronic; their sound was both ancient and new. Heavy metal is popular throughout the world because it issues from a prehistoric source that we all share. Heavy metal has been reinvented by generations of angry teenagers because there have always been angry teenagers. Dionysus and Apollo are two old gods who survived into the modern world to inspire the

Black Sabbath and Philosophy: Mastering Reality, First Edition. Edited by William Irwin.
© 2013 John Wiley & Sons, Inc. Published 2013 by John Wiley & Sons, Inc.

development of new art—especially art that is terrifying and awe inspiring and dark and scary and fueled by wine and other intoxicants.

Let's meet those gods. Let's hear their stories. Let's honor their power.

In Praise of Sweet Leaf and COKE-Cola

The German philosopher Friedrich Nietzsche (1844–1900) wrote in *Twilight of the Idols: Or, How to Philosophize with the Hammer* that intoxication heightens artistic sensibility and makes art possible. There are many different ways of becoming intoxicated: sex, great cravings, strong emotions, festivals, competition, daredevilry, victory, extreme commotion, cruelty, destruction, spring, drugs, and "the intoxication of an overloaded and swollen will."[1] Drugs are the part of the list most relevant to our story. Drugs may not be safe or legal, but many artists agree with Nietzsche that a narcotic-induced intoxication can heighten sensitivity and make art possible.

From the beginning of Black Sabbath, Ozzy, Tony, Bill, and Geezer used drugs in rock-and-roll-myth-making amounts. Ozzy's autobiography, *I am Ozzy*, starts with this footnote:

> *Other people's memories of the stuff in this book might not be the same as mine. I ain't gonna argue with 'em. Over the past forty years I've been loaded on booze, coke, acid, Quaaludes, glue, cough mixture, heroin, Rohypnol, Klonopin, Vicodin, and too many other heavy-duty substances to list in this footnote. On more than a few occasions I was on all of those at the same time. I'm not the fucking *Encyclopaedia Britannica*, put it that way. What you read here is what dribbled out of the jelly I call my brain when I asked it for my life story. Nothing more, nothing less . . . .[2]

As a teenager working in a car-part manufacturing plant (and so years before forming Black Sabbath), Ozzy would sniff the methylene chloride in "a big fucking degreasing machine" that gave an intoxication "like sniffing glue . . . times a fucking hundred."[3] Each founding member of Black Sabbath brought with them a habit of pursuing intoxication through alcohol and drugs. Ozzy writes that drummer Bill Ward liked to drink a cider that "was like having a head injury."[4] And about bassist Geezer Butler, Ozzy writes: "When I first met him he was also smoking a lot of dope. You'd be out with him at a club, say, and he'd start talking about wormholes in the vibration of consciousness, or some other fucking loony shit."[5] Much like the Beatles before them, the young Black Sabbath got an enormous amount of training playing all day at the Star-Club in Hamburg, Germany. About the experience, Ozzy writes: "It was a lot of fun, but it was fucking grueling, man. Every day we'd start at noon and end at two in the morning. You'd do speed, pills, dope, beer—anything you could lay your hands on—just to stay awake."[6]

Guitarist Tony Iommi is the unofficial leader of Black Sabbath and the sole continuous member. In his autobiography, *Iron Man: My Journey Through Heaven and Hell with Black Sabbath*, Tony writes about those early days in Hamburg: "We were smoking dope there a lot and I was pretty pie-eyed." He also explains Bill's method of preparing banana peels for smoking: "He used to eat the banana, scrape all the residue off the skin, put it on to a piece of tin foil, put that in the oven, cook it and then smoke it. He claimed it got him high, thought it was great and was really proud of it."[7] Concerning their second album, *Paranoid*, Tony writes: "We smoked a lot of dope, so that might be why some of the lyrics are a bit unusual."[8] Tony writes that during the recording of the third album, *Master of Reality*, Ozzy brought him "a bloody big joint" and "I coughed my head off, they taped that and we used it on the beginning of 'Sweet Leaf'. How appropriate: coughing your way into a song about marijuana . . . and the finest vocal performance of my entire career!"[9] Tony especially enjoyed recording *Vol. 4* and writes: "That whole period was one of the most enjoyable times ever, and a song like 'Snowblind' makes it clear that it was also because of a certain drug. That's why we wrote on the album sleeve 'We wish to thank the great COKE-Cola Company'."[10]

The band tended to avoid more solitary and dangerous drugs like heroin, which they warn against in "Hand of Doom." In his autobiography, Ozzy writes "when heroin gets hold of you, it's usually The End."[11] And despite Sabbath's love of cocaine, "Snowblind" clearly depicts an addict in denial. On the downsides of cocaine use, Ozzy notes that it makes everything you say seem "like the most fabulous thing you've ever heard in your life,"[12] but then you try to say fabulous things for "fifteen hours straight"[13] until the epiglottis hanging in your throat "is the size of a small light bulb"[14] and your heart is beating at "eight times its usual speed"[15] and it "twists your whole idea of reality" and "you start seeing things that aren't there" and then Tony walks off stage at the Hollywood Bowl and collapses "after doing coke literally for days."[16]

The Birth of Tragedy and the Birth of Heavy Metal

In 1872 (when he was at that dangerous age of twenty-seven[17]), Nietzsche published his first book: *The Birth of Tragedy*.[18] People hated it. Scholars liked to think of the ancient Athenians as cultured and refined people who were decent and mannered while they created reverent plays for the stage. But Nietzsche argued that those plays had their origins in men drinking wine together and singing songs. The very idea that the theater could come from groups of drunken singers seemed preposterous to the stuffy German professors of 1872. But I think Nietzsche was right. The famous playwrights Aeschylus (525–456 BCE) and Sophocles (496–406 BCE) did something new by having actors who stepped out of the chorus and gave lines of dialogue. Actors were an innovation because the older form of theater was to simply have a chorus—which is a group of men singing and dancing in unison. In their plays, Aeschylus and Sophocles still included a chorus that sings and interacts with the actors on the stage. The chorus came first. Men singing together. Alcohol must have been involved because the ancient Athenian playwrights were competing for awards during the Dionysian Festival, and Dionysus is the ancient Greek god of intoxication.

Nietzsche argues in *The Birth of Tragedy* that a synthesis of the drinking together, the celebration of Dionysus, the influence of the visual plastic arts (painting and sculpture), and the terrifying images of Apollo made possible the wonderful ancient Athenian creation of tragic theater. Contemporary theorist Camille Paglia extends Nietzsche's thesis beyond the Greeks in her book *Sexual Personae: Art and Decadence from Nefertiti to Emily Dickinson*.[19] Paglia argues that a synthesis of Dionysus and Apollo can also be found in Shakespeare, Blake, Goethe, Wordsworth, Coleridge, Byron, Keats, and others. In her *Sex, Art, and American Culture*, Paglia writes about Dionysus and Apollo in Hollywood movies, rock music, and drag queens.[20] Personally, I think that Dionysus and Apollo were there with Black Sabbath at the birth of heavy metal.

Listening to a heavy metal album or attending a heavy metal concert or thrashing in a mosh pit or playing in a heavy metal band is participating in a modern, electronic Dionysian festival. Heavy metal is horrific: Black Sabbath lyrics deal with death, fear, magic, and more—yet this is what we love about the songs. Heavy metal is loud: it is easy to lose yourself in the sheer volume. And heavy metal is about bands: groups of people working together toward a common goal of pleasure. These are the characteristics of Dionysus and Apollo. So now let's meet Dionysus. Later we'll visit Apollo.

Goat Songs and Clowns

The word "tragedy" means "goat song"—a reference to the cloven goat feet of Dionysus and the satyrs. Nietzsche writes that the ancient theater offered many opportunities for losing oneself. The artist loses himself in the characters as he writes the play. The actors lose themselves in the characters as they perform the play. And the audience lose themselves in the characters as they watch the play. As we watch with pity and fear for the characters on the stage, we the audience feel that we are not alone in the horrors of existence that we experience. Make no mistake about it, the Athenian plays were horrific. Queen Clytemnestra kills her husband Agamemnon on his first day home from the Trojan War; Medea drowns her own children; Oedipus gouges out his own eyes after seeing his mother/wife hang herself. And yet, paradoxically, through these artistic representations of the worst horrors of existence, we enjoy life. We experience a catharsis, a purging of fear and pity.[21]

Dionysus is famously the god of wine, but he is more than that because wine entails so much. The god of wine is the god of cultivating the grape vine—watching it die each fall and be reborn each spring. For a distant pleasure, grape cultivation requires labor and extended cooperation among people. And the pleasure of wine includes singing, dancing, throwing some meat on the fire, and having a party. Drunken parties can lead to all sorts of things . . . Wine can create a group party, group singing, group sex,[22] group hangovers, and group madness. An intoxicated person, through Dionysus, can belong to a group and lose the troubling self. Loneliness can be painful. An individual sometimes feels so lonely that he thinks no one understands him. But Dionysus is the god of losing your individuality in a reveling party where everyone understands because they've been drinking it too.

The members of Black Sabbath know about the pain of isolation and loneliness because everyone knows about the pain of isolation and loneliness. But you don't have to be alone. There really are others like you. They put it best in "Sabbath Bloody Sabbath": "They just tell you that you're on your own / Fill your head all full of lies." The lie is that you have to be on your own. The lie of the "self-made man." The lie of the rugged individual. It's not true. You don't have to be on your own. There is always a community to join. I joined the heavy metal community as a teenager and smoked my first joint at an Ozzy Osbourne concert in 1986. (I was part of a small community of metal snobs who were there to see the opening band: Metallica on their *Master of Puppets* tour with Cliff Burton in bellbottoms still playing the bass. And I really did feel good being a member of a community who got this music while the mainstream didn't. It felt so cool.)

Black Sabbath has worked through enormous setbacks: guitarist amputates fingertips, bass player on LSD, drummer on fire, lead singer misses show because passed out in the wrong hotel room on cold medicine and who knows what else. This would have killed lesser bands and mere mortals, but the members of Black Sabbath have survived and thrived. Ozzy, Tony, Geezer, and Bill have a bond that is "as close as any heterosexual men can be" as they say in the interview on the DVD *The Last Supper*. And much of this has been fueled by drug use.

Ozzy's drug use is part of his class clown persona. In *I Am Ozzy* he describes being pushed around by bullies as a kid and being beaten by abusive teachers. Clowning became his survival mechanism because the bully wouldn't hit you if they were laughing at you. Ozzy will do anything for a laugh; he's been conditioned to clown around to be accepted. In competition with rival clowns, this becomes daredevilry—what Ozzy calls "trying to out-crazy one another." Ozzy had daredevil clown rivalries with John Bonham (drummer for Led Zeppelin)[23] and the entire band of Mötley Crüe (during the *Bark at the Moon* tour). Who can drink the most? Who can smoke the most? Who loves to snort so much that they would snort ants?[24] Ozzy brings his clown persona to the stage—he knows how to work an audience into a frenzy, and if all else fails he'll show his ass. The audience participates, gets involved, frequently while intoxicated. At a Sabbath concert you are part of a group of like minded crazy metal heads who love things turned up to 11. Ozzy, Tony, Geezer, and Bill found an extended family in Black Sabbath. Many people find a tribe in rock bands. To a lesser extent the fans can participate by being a member of a tribe. We can be part of the heavy metal community. The experience can be a communal experience and can overcome loneliness and existential despair.

A Satanic Interlude

Nietzsche writes about the importance of the Satyr chorus in ancient Athenian tragedies. Satyrs are wild goat men who walk with goat legs and cloven feet and sport goat horns on their grinning heads. Satyrs are horny and love to chase nymphs and even goats. Satyrs are the companions of Dionysus. Nietzsche writes that we can identify with the Satyrs (who are certainly more like us than those distant gods!), and in turn the Satyrs provide justification for our life.[25] We enjoy drinking and getting horny just like the Satyrs do. However, through Christianity, these goat men became the model for Satan with his cloven hooves, tail, and horns. When we look at heavy metal iconography, we need to look past the Christian view of those satanic images and see the Satyrs from the days long before Christianity.

If Nietzsche Had Been a Black Sabbath Fan

No one writes like Nietzsche. An essay about Nietzsche tames him, cleans him up, trims his moustache, and makes him presentable. But Nietzsche's writing is wild, and reading him is a rush. Here is my attempt at recreating that rush. If Nietzsche had been a Black Sabbath fan he would have written:

1

He who fights with the Wizard must see to it that he himself not become a Wizard. And when you gaze long into the Wicked World, the Wicked World stares back at you.[26]

2

Have you not read of the *Diary of a Madman*? He ran into the streets during the daylight hours crying, "Iron Man is dead, and we have killed him—you and I. All of us are his murderers. But how did we do it? How did we kill Iron Man? Who could clean our hands of his murder? Must we ourselves become Iron Men to be worthy of such a deed?"[27]

3

From the Ozzy school of life.—That which gets me higher makes me stronger.[28]

4

What? Was Dio Black Sabbath's mistake? Or was Black Sabbath Dio's mistake?[29]

5

How little it takes to make us happy ... the sound of a power chord! Without heavy metal, life would be unbearable. I can even imagine that God sings along to Black Sabbath.[30]

6

Formula for my happiness: a riff, a base line, drums, and *evil lyrics* . . .[31]

7

Whatever is heard on *Sabbath Bloody Sabbath* always occurs beyond good and evil.[32]

8

Metal bands are rarely just individuals—but in groups, parties, nations, and ages they totally rule.[33]

9

A man with a guitar is unbearable if he does not also have at least two other things: killer riffs and *Marshall* amps.[34]

10

The metal head.—He is a metal head; that means, he knows how to make things louder than they are.[35]

11

The heaviest metal.—What good is heavy metal that does not even carry us beyond all heavy metal?[36]

What Is This That Stands Before Me?

There's more ... There's Apollo—a totally different god. Nietzsche writes in *The Birth of Tragedy* that Apollo originally inspired the plastic artist who sculpts or paints images from dreams and visions.

Apollo is famously the ancient Greek god of the sun, but he is also the god of dreams and visions. Apollo is a frightening god, for he is the god of pestilence, archery (death from a distance!), the burning Sun, and of individual madness: of epileptics, of blind soothsayers, of cursed prophetesses. The opening line of "Black Sabbath" is straight-up Apollo: "What is this that stands before me? / Figure in black which points at me." Terrified, Ozzy screams for God's help while Tony Iommi plays the frightening *diabolus in musica*: dum – DUM – dumumumumumumumumumum …. Apollo terrified the ancient Greeks. Apollo is strange, for he is depicted as a slender but muscular man whose beardless face can seem boyish. But this young god terrified people. His Priestess (the "Pythian") at the famous Oracle of Delphi would inhale noxious fumes, enter a strange hypnotic trance, and speak terrifying prophecies as the voice of Apollo. I know of no ancient Greek author who wrote about their love of Apollo. They write of his terrors. In Homer's *Iliad*, Apollo fights for the Trojans against the Greeks. I feel Apollo's ancient terror in metal with its images of inverted crosses, devil babies, and the Prince of Darkness.

Tony Iommi has often remarked that he believes there is a fifth member of the band—a phantom presence. Tony's *Iron Man: My Journey through Heaven and Hell with Black Sabbath* has many stories of ghosts, dream images, and angels. Here are some of them:

- A teenage Tony flips his MGB sports car (a convertible with no roll bars!). "It sounds mad, but I saw three figures come down, one to the left and two to the right, like angels. And I thought, this is it."[37]
- Tony was in the band Mythology with Bill Ward prior to Black Sabbath. One night they counted heads for ordering fish and chips. They counted one too many because they included the ghost of a young boy who had a "bad death" many years ago in that flat.[38]
- Each member of Black Sabbath once dreamed the same dream of wearing crosses to protect them from evil, and then they started doing so.[39]
- While living in a 200-room mansion, Tony sees a ghost walk up the stairs and a poltergeist steals his keys, knocks some paintings, and opens his briefcase.[40]
- Still in the same mansion, Tony reads Lobsang Rampa and begins experimenting with astral projection.[41]

- The band rented Clearwell Castle for inspiration for their fifth album. Tony and Geezer see a black figure headed towards the armory. This leads to ghost stories and pranks. The owner of the castle claims that a maid mourning her dead baby haunts it. Tony writes "Sabbath Bloody Sabbath" on their first day of work in Clearwell Castle.[42]

What does this mean? Tony Iommi tells many stories of phantoms, ghosts, angels, and visions. They are always apparitions of people. He never sees octopus-headed Cthulu-style creatures. Iommi has visions of people who are either covered in black clothing or young and beautiful. They are like Apollo who is always depicted as a beautiful beardless youth.

Geezer Butler has the most famous Black Sabbath apparition story. Apparently Geezer painted his whole bedroom black with inverted crosses, and Ozzy lent him an old book about the occult. That night Geezer saw a figure in black standing before his bed. When he awoke, the old book was gone. Ozzy sings about Geezer's experience in Black Sabbath's "Black Sabbath" on *Black Sabbath*. Right at the heart of the origin of heavy metal is a horror story about a nighttime bedroom visitor—the figure in black—Geezer's apparition from Ozzy's occult book—Apollo—the awesome, fearsome, frightening, terrifying son of Zeus.

Nietzsche argued that a synthesis of the group drinking, singing of Dionysus, and terrifying images of Apollo made the ancient Athenian tragedies possible. I think we can also find the gods in Black Sabbath and the origin of heavy metal. Black Sabbath was a group of men drinking and smoking and snorting and playing loud music together with frightening lyrics of visions and nightmares and madness. Enough said.

Warning: Not for Mere Mortals

This is dangerous stuff. This stuff can kill you, or worse. In "Fairies Wear Boots," Ozzy sings, "So I went to the doctor, see what he could give me / He said son, son, you've gone too far / 'Cause smokin' and trippin' is all that you do.'" Listen to Bill Ward discuss addiction in the 1999 DVD *The Last Supper*. That's frightening. Or just listen to

Ozzy speak. That's what this stuff will do to you. Ozzy's survival might just be due to his genetics. In *Trust Me, I'm Dr. Ozzy: Advice from Rock's Ultimate Survivor* he discusses the recent mapping of his genome. A group of scientists told him: "you've said it yourself: you're a *medical miracle*. You went on a drink and drugs bender for 40 years. You broke your neck on a quad bike. You died twice in a chemically induced coma. You walked away from your tour bus without a scratch after it was hit by a plane. Your immune system was so compromised by your lifestyle, you got a positive HIV test for 24 hours, until they proved it was wrong. And yet here you are, alive and well and living in Buckinghamshire."[43] Even Tony Iommi remarks that Ozzy always had the unhealthiest lifestyle of anyone in Black Sabbath and yet he always seemed to be the healthiest.[44] Ozzy isn't a normal person. If you don't have Ozzy's genetic makeup, then you probably couldn't survive his life. Don't try.[45]

Notes

1. *"Towards a psychology of the artist.*—For there to be art, for there to be any aesthetic activity and observation, one physiological prerequisite is indispensable: *intoxication*. Intoxication must already have heightened the sensitivity of the whole machine: otherwise, no art will be forthcoming. All kinds of intoxication, as different as their causes may be, have this power: above all, the intoxication of sexual excitement, that oldest most primordial form of intoxication. Likewise the intoxication that follows all great cravings, all strong emotions; the intoxication of the festival, of the competition, of daredevilry, of victory, of every extreme commotion; the intoxication of cruelty; the intoxication of destruction; intoxication due to certain meteorological influences, such as the intoxication of spring; or under the influence of narcotics; finally, the intoxication of the will, the intoxication of an overloaded and swollen will.—

   What is essential in intoxication is the feeling of increased strength and fullness. This feeling leads us to donate to things, to *make* them take from us, to force ourselves on them—this process is called *idealizing*. Let's get rid of a prejudice at this point: idealizing does *not* consist, as is commonly thought, in taking away or subtracting what is small and incidental. Instead, what is decisive is an immense drive to *bring out* the principal traits, so that the others disappear in the process," Friedrich Nietzsche, *Twilight of the Idols: Or, How to Philosophize with the Hammer*, trans. Richard Polt (Indianapolis: Hackett, 1997), 55, § 8.

2. Ozzy Osbourne with Chris Ayres, *I Am Ozzy* (New York: Grand Central, 2009).

3. Ibid., 26.

4. Ibid., 77.

5. Ibid., 50.

6. Ibid., 86.

7. Tony Iommi with T.J. Lammers, *Iron Man: My Journey Through Heaven and Hell with Black Sabbath* (Cambridge, MA: Da Capo Press, 2011), 57–59.

8. Ibid., 73.

9. Ibid., 95.

10. Ibid., 113.

11. *I Am Ozzy*, 139.

12. "It would be almost impossible to exaggerate how much coke we did in that house. We'd discovered that when you take coke, every thought you have, every word you say, every suggestion you make seems like the most fabulous thing you've ever heard in your life," *I Am Ozzy*, 130.

13. "The constant fear of getting busted wasn't the only downside to coke. It got to the point where practically every word out of my mouth was coked-up bollocks. For fifteen hours straight, I'd tell the lads how much I loved them more than anything else in the world. Even me and Tony—who *never* had conversations—would have nights when we'd be up for hours, hugging each other and saying, 'No, really, I love you man—I *really* love you'," *I Am Ozzy*, 138.

14. A doctor on Sunset Boulevard looked down Ozzy's throat and said: "Mr. Osbourne, your epiglottis is the size of a small light bulb, and it's glowing almost as brightly. I don't even need to use my flashlight," *I Am Ozzy*, 140.

15. "Then I'd go to bed, wait for my heart to stop beating at eight times its usual speed, then fall into this fucking horrific withdrawal," *I Am Ozzy*, 139.

16. "Even Tony burned out. Just after we'd finished the album (*Vol. 4*), we did a gig at the Hollywood Bowl. Tony had been doing coke literally for days—we all had, but Tony had gone over the edge. I mean, that stuff just twists your whole idea of reality. You start seeing things that aren't there. And Tony was *gone*. Near the end of the gig he walked off the stage and collapsed," *I Am Ozzy*, 139.

17. Twenty-seven is a dangerous age for drug and alcohol abuse. The members of the 27 club are famous musicians who died at 27, mostly from heroin or alcohol abuse: Robert Johnson (look him up!), Brian Jones, Jimi Hendrix, Janis Joplin, Jim Morrison, Kurt Cobain, and recently Amy Winehouse, who sang: "They tried to make me go to rehab, but I said NO, NO, NO!"

18. Friedrich Nietzsche, *The Birth of Tragedy and The Case of Wagner*, trans. Walter Kaufmann (New York: Vintage, 1967), "Translator's Introduction," 4.

19. Camille Paglia, *Sexual Personae: Art and Decadence from Nefertiti to Emily Dickenson* (New York: Vintage, 1991).

20. Camille Paglia, *Sex, Art, and American Culture* (New York: Vintage, 1992).

21. For more on catharsis see my "Why We Enjoy Reading about Men Who Hate Women: Aristotle's Cathartic Appeal," in Eric Bronson, ed., *The Girl with the Dragon Tattoo and Philosophy: Everything is Fire* (Hoboken: John Wiley & Sons, 2012), 120–127.

22. Ozzy writes about the scene at the pool in a Holiday Inn during the *Paranoid* tour: "It was like *Caligula* up there: dozens of the most amazing-looking chicks you could ever imagine, all stark naked, and blowjobs and threesomes going on left, right, and center. I lit up a joint, sat down on a recliner between two lesbian chicks, and began to sing 'God Bless America'," *I Am Ozzy*, 120.

23. "After a few nights out with Zeppelin, I worked out that their drummer, John Bonham, was as fucking nuts as I was, so we'd spend most of the time trying to out-crazy each other. That was always the way with me, y'know? I'd try to win people over with my craziness, like I had in the playground at Birchfield Road. But, of course, behind the mask there was a sad old clown most of the time. Bonham was the same, I think. He would just drink himself to fucking bits," *I Am Ozzy*, 147–148.

24. Ozzy will neither confirm nor deny snorting a line of ants during the *Bark at the Moon* tour while he was trying to "out crazy" the opening band Mötley Crüe: "People tell me stories about that tour and I have no idea if they're true or not. They ask, 'Ozzy, did you really once snort a line of ants off a Popsicle stick?' and I ain't got a fucking clue. It's certainly possible. Every night stuff went up my nose that had no business being there. I was out of it the whole time," *I Am Ozzy*, 262.

25. "In this magic transformation the Dionysian reveler sees himself as a satyr, *and as a satyr, in turn, he sees the god*, which means that in his metamorphosis he beholds another vision outside himself, as the Apollonian complement of his own state," Nietzsche, *The Birth of Tragedy*, 64, § 8.

26. "Whoever fights monsters should see to it that in the process he does not become a monster. And when you look long into an abyss, the abyss also looks into you," Nietzsche, *Beyond Good and Evil: Prelude to a Philosophy of the Future*, trans. Walter Kaufmann (New York: Vintage, 1989), 89, § 146.

27. Nietzsche's original includes his famous "God is dead" statement. It is too long to quote fully here, but starts as: "*The madman.*—Have you not heard of that madman who lit a lantern in the bright morning hours, ran to the marketplace and cried incessantly: 'I seek God! I seek God!'," Nietzsche, *The Gay Science: With a Prelude in Rhymes and an Appendix of Songs*, trans. Walter Kaufmann (New York: Vintage, 1974), 181, § 125.

28. "*From life's military school.*—What doesn't kill me makes me stronger," Nietzsche, *Twilight of the Idols*, 6, § 8.

29. "What? Is humanity just God's mistake? Or God just a mistake of humanity?—," Nietzsche, *Twilight of the Idols*, 6, § 7.

30. "How little it takes to make us happy! The sound of a bagpipe.— Without music, life would be an error. The German even imagines God as singing songs," Nietzsche, *Twilight of the Idols*, 10, § 33.

31. "Formula for my happiness: a yes, a no, a straight line, a *goal* . . .," Nietzsche, *Twilight of the Idols*, 11, § 44.

32. "Whatever is done from love always occurs beyond good and evil," Nietzsche, *Beyond Good and Evil*, 90, § 153.

33. "Madness is rare in individuals—but in groups, parties, nations, and ages it is the rule," Nietzsche, *Beyond Good and Evil*, 90, § 156.

34. "A man with spirit is unbearable if he does not also have at least two other things: gratitude and cleanliness," Nietzsche, *Beyond Good and Evil*, 80, § 74.

35. "*The thinker.*—He is a thinker; that means, he knows how to make things simpler than they are," Nietzsche, *The Gay Science*, 205, § 189.

36. "*Books.*—What good is a book that does not even carry us beyond all books?," Nietzsche, *The Gay Science*, 215, § 248.

37. *Iron Man*, 33.

38. Ibid., 36

39. Ibid., 81.

40. Ibid., 120–121.

41. Ibid., 121.

42. Ibid., 130–132.

43. Ozzy Osbourne, with Chris Ayres, *Trust Me, I'm Dr. Ozzy: Advice from Rock's Ultimate Survivor* (New York: Grand Central, 2011), 142. Thank you to my sister's wife, Rebecca Bunner, for loaning me a fucking autographed copy of this!

44. *Iron Man*, 103–104.

45. Thank you, Jennifer McCarthy, my lovely wife, for the many helpful suggestions on multiple drafts. Thank you, Bill Irwin, for this opportunity and the encouragement. Thank you, all the metalheads I've known, especially Mike Knepp and Chris Magerkurth. Check out www.mapofmetal.com to see this incredible world Black Sabbath spawned.

Part IV

IS IT STILL SABBATH WITHOUT OZZY?

Chapter 11

It's Not Sabbath Unless Ozzy's the Singer (But It's Fine If You Disagree)

James Bondarchuk

Black Sabbath arose from the working-class ashes of Birmingham, England in 1968. The original "Sab Four" included guitarist Tony Iommi, bassist Terry "Geezer" Butler, drummer Bill Ward, and a 20-year-old ex-burglar and aspiring singer named John "Ozzy" Osbourne. Together they created a style of music that was significantly heavier, darker, and more powerful than that of their immediate predecessors in Cream or colleagues in Led Zeppelin and Deep Purple. For a solid decade this motley cast of Black Country brummies pushed hard rock to new heights of heaviness, but internal tensions and changing circumstances precipitated a series of line-up changes. While no doubt the most significant of these changes was the replacement of Ozzy Osbourne by Ronnie James Dio in 1979, it was far from the only one. To date, at least 30 people have been considered "members" of Black Sabbath, with founding member Tony Iommi the only constant presence in the band.[1]

Despite these line-up changes, one thing is for sure: hard rock and metal fans take their Sabbath very seriously. For many, myself included, Black Sabbath is not just another hard rock or metal band; they are the soundtrack of our inner lives, heaviness distilled, the archetype for all the Judas Priests and Iron Maidens that followed. Only trouble is, when it comes to the post-Ozzy line-ups, we Sabbath fans can't seem to agree on much. Many—the "purists"

Black Sabbath and Philosophy: Mastering Reality, First Edition. Edited by William Irwin.
© 2013 John Wiley & Sons, Inc. Published 2013 by John Wiley & Sons, Inc.

among us—insist that only the group consisting of the four original members is the true Black Sabbath. Others are willing to acknowledge that the band helmed by Ronnie James Dio into the early 1980s was an authentic continuation of Black Sabbath, but draw the line there. And a small but vocal minority of fans insist that later groups that recorded as Black Sabbath—including ones in which guitarist Tony Iommi was the sole remaining original member—were the genuine article. But which of these bands were really Black Sabbath, and which, if any, were merely Sabbath in name only?

I am firmly in the purist camp. Don't get me wrong; I really enjoy some of the later albums, but they just do not feel like Sabbath to me, and I wish they had been released under different names. For my money, Sabbath will always be identified with the four original members and the eight groundbreaking studio albums they recorded together in the 1970s. But despite being an outspoken purist, I have some sympathy for the arguments that non-purists regularly put forward. All of us—purists and non-purists alike—deserve to present our case before what the philosopher Immanuel Kant (1724–1804) called the "court of reason."[2] With this in mind, I hope to shed some light on this debate by appealing to the standards and methods of philosophy.

Mastering Metaphysical Reality: Why Geezer Butler Isn't a Plank of Wood

Philosophers often want to get a sense of the kind of question they are trying to answer, in the hope that doing so will provide insight into how they might go about answering it. If we're not clear about the kind of question we're trying to answer, we're just going to end up spinning the wheels of our own confusion. For instance, many ordinary questions can be settled by simple observation, but the question concerning whether some group of musicians is "really" Black Sabbath isn't such a question. Sure, we can observe whether these musicians ever toured as "Black Sabbath," whether they ever recorded an album under that name, and so forth; but any such observation we make will have to be informed by some prior principle for deciding whether that observation is relevant to our question. For instance, suppose you say, "Ronnie James Dio was a member of Black Sabbath. After all, he is listed as the singer in the liner notes to *Heaven and Hell*, and that album clearly says 'Black Sabbath' on the cover." Of course, no one disputes that Dio sang on that album or that it was released under the name "Black Sabbath." What people disagree about is the implicit principle you've relied on—that releasing an album under the name "Black Sabbath" makes you a member of Black Sabbath, or what amounts to the same, that a line-up that records as "Black Sabbath" is, in fact, Black Sabbath. The upshot is that we need a principle for settling the question of whether any such group is Black Sabbath or not—and that's not the kind of thing that could be settled by observation alone. Instead, it will require a bit of philosophical inquiry.

Minimally, such a principle would have to specify what philosophers call "necessary" and "sufficient" conditions for whether a band is Black Sabbath. If a group of musicians fails to satisfy the necessary conditions, then that group is not Black Sabbath; if a different group satisfies the sufficient conditions, then it is. We combine the notions of necessary and sufficient conditions in the thought that a band counts as a genuine instance of Black Sabbath "if and only if" certain conditions are satisfied.

Such a principle might still be inadequate for our purposes, however, because if such a principle were able to determine *whether* a particular band is Black Sabbath, it might leave us wondering *why* that band is or is not Black Sabbath. To be able to answer the latter question, we need to know what Black Sabbath is essentially. This takes us into the branch of philosophy called metaphysics, which is concerned with the ultimate nature of reality. Traditionally, metaphysicians concerned themselves with such lofty questions as whether God exists or whether human beings possess freedom of the will. We are concerned with a question that, to at least some, will seem no less important: the ultimate nature of Black Sabbath.

Since we're thinking about the metaphysics of Black Sabbath, it might be helpful to see how this problem compares to similar metaphysical questions. You might think our question really amounts to this: how many members of Black Sabbath can we replace before we have an altogether different band? More specifically, what is the relation of the "parts" (the individual members) of the band at any given time to the identity of the "whole" (the band itself) across time? When we put the question this way, it resembles a classic philosophical problem known as the "Ship of Theseus Paradox," which was originally posed by the Greek thinker Plutarch (ca 45–120 CE).

Suppose we replaced one plank on a wooden ship. We are disposed to judge that the resulting ship is the same ship as before—that it is identical with the preceding one. This is because we generally think that by replacing a single plank of wood, we don't thereby change the identity of the ship; it's the same ship as before.

Now, suppose we replaced another plank of wood. According to the principle that says that by replacing one plank of wood we retain the same ship, we must conclude that the resulting ship is identical with the preceding one. Notice, however, that by repeating this process and replacing the planks one-by-one we will eventually have a ship whose parts are altogether different from that of the original ship. But now we face the following problem: how can two ships whose material parts are altogether different from each other—the one we started with and the one we ended with—be the same ship?

Even if this question doesn't worry us and we accept that the resulting ship is identical with the original one, the English philosopher Thomas Hobbes (1588–1679) pointed out that we now face an even more difficult problem. Suppose we gathered up all of the original planks of wood and built a ship from them. Would *that* ship be identical with the one we started with? Intuitively, we think that a ship built in the same fashion out of all of the original planks of wood must be identical with the original one. But now that means we have two non-identical ships both of which are identical to the original one—an evident contradiction. We can see that Hobbes's example threatens the very plausible assumption that we can replace a single plank of wood and preserve the identity of the ship.[3] Perhaps we're better off saying that we cannot retain the same ship by replacing one of its planks. In a similar way, we might say that we cannot retain the same band by replacing any of its members.

Unfortunately for our purposes, the two cases seem to evoke very different beliefs. Before we tangle ourselves up in metaphysical knots trying to solve these problems, we are generally apt to judge that we can preserve the identity of a ship by replacing one of its planks. By contrast, we are generally less disposed to think that we can preserve the identity of a band by replacing any individual member. This suggests that the planks from our example do not play a role exactly analogous to that of the members of a band. A plank of wood has a certain well-defined function in the composition of a ship, and it can be easily replaced by another object as long as that object performs that same function. But to the extent that it's even appropriate to speak of an individual musician's having a certain "function" within a band, we don't generally think that a musician's primary value or contribution is the kind of thing that can be so easily replaced. A musician brings a particular style to bear in his or her playing or performing, a style that is the culmination and expression of that musician's influences and experiences.

This ineliminable human component doesn't really fit the model presented to us by Theseus's ship. By trying to imagine "N.I.B." without the low end of Geezer's fluid bass lines, or "Electric Funeral" without Ozzy's characteristic wail, we see at once how important these particular individuals are to the essence of, if not Black Sabbath, then at least these songs. By saying this I don't mean to assume that these musicians could never be replaced without fundamentally altering what is essential about Black Sabbath. I just mean to say that we need to look elsewhere for a comparison. Although he might not have Ozzy's animated personality, there is at least one respect in which Geezer Butler is unlike a wooden plank.

Perhaps organizations like nation-states or sports teams provide a better basis for comparison, since they are constituted by persons instead of planks. But again, such comparisons tend to evoke the wrong beliefs. After all, it is expected that the players on a sports team (or the citizens of a political body) will eventually be replaced or die out. No one who claims "I have been a die-hard Yankees fan my whole life and I always will be" identifies the Yankees with any particular roster of players, and if our imagined fan is fortunate, she will live long enough to see her beloved Yankees with a completely different collection of players. (Moreover, anyone who has listened to a few minutes of sports radio will be acquainted with the zeal with which certain fans are willing to trade and fire players for the betterment of the "team.") By contrast, it is not generally expected that the members of a band will eventually be replaced. In particular, almost no one believes that a band without any original members could be a genuine version of Black Sabbath.

Behind the Wall of Thought Experiments

Since looking to other bases for comparison hasn't seemed too promising, I propose we subject to philosophical scrutiny the principles and maxims most frequently cited by actual Sabbath fans to support their beliefs about which line-ups were really Sabbath. We will proceed by devising what philosophers call "thought experiments." These are experiments of a special sort—the kind we can perform simply by thinking hard about a problem. We can "test" each principle by determining where it stands on particular cases, including crazy scenarios that we devise in our heads, and seeing whether each principle agrees with our beliefs. An initially plausible principle might have to be rejected because it gives what we consider to be an obviously wrong answer on some scenario that we devise. (We've already seen an example of this with the Ship of Theseus Paradox.) By proceeding in this way we might shed some light on the essence of Black Sabbath and reach some positive conclusion about Sabbath's identity.

To start with the most obvious (and popular) principle: *a band is Black Sabbath if and only if it comprises the four original members of Black Sabbath*. This is the principle most often cited by the purists who insist that Sabbath ceased to exist during the years that Ozzy was not in the band. We might read this principle as just an instantiation of the more general principle that says that a band consists of its original members only, and any line-up changes result in an altogether different band. More specifically, such a principle states that *for any band X, a band Y is identical with X if and only if the members of Y are all and only the original members of X*. However, while this principle might be true in the case of Sabbath, it is apt to clash with our intuitions about the identities of other bands.

For instance, according to the more general principle, Metallica was no longer "really" Metallica after Ron McGovney, their original bassist, was fired from the band and replaced by Cliff Burton. Of course, McGovney did not play on any of the early studio albums that defined Metallica's sound. We might get around this objection by identifying (somewhat arbitrarily) the members of a band with those individuals who performed on a band's first album. But again, the principle overreaches. For according to it, Bruce Dickinson was never a member of Iron Maiden, since the principle implies that a band is Iron Maiden only if Paul Di'Anno (who performed on Maiden's first two albums, and who was replaced by Bruce Dickinson) is a member. (Many if not most Maiden fans consider the version of the band helmed by Dickinson to be its classic line-up.)

If instead we interpret this principle as saying something specific about Black Sabbath—that while some other bands can have their original members replaced and retain their identity as a band, Sabbath cannot—we run into a different problem: it does not explain why Black Sabbath is necessarily constituted by its original members while those other bands aren't. The principle might then be true, but utterly unilluminating as to the essence or identity of Black Sabbath. Moreover—and this is where a little thought experimentation comes in handy—let's suppose the four original members of Black Sabbath decided to tour under a totally different name and play nothing but piano covers of Justin Bieber songs. The proposed principle implies that *that* band would still be Black Sabbath. To some (myself included) this would be a *reductio ad absurdum* of the principle. Therefore, as far as this principle is concerned, this is one case where the mob doesn't rule.

This might suggest that *a band is Black Sabbath if and only if (1) it comprises the four original members of Black Sabbath, (2) it records or tours under the name "Black Sabbath," and (3) it plays or records music consistent with Black Sabbath's musical style.* As a purist about Black Sabbath, I find myself in agreement with this principle the most. However, there are at least two problems with it. The first is that the original members themselves reject condition (2) by claiming to have started Black Sabbath in 1968, even though they did not change their name to "Black Sabbath" until late in 1969.[4] Nonetheless, we might not think this is such a big problem, since our governing concern need not be fealty to the band members' personal attitudes about the matter; after all, they are musicians, not metaphysicians.

However, a second, deeper problem with this principle is that the third condition's appeal to Black Sabbath's "style" covertly evokes some notion of what is essential about Black Sabbath's music. Thus our revised principle seems to smuggle in some notion about Sabbath's essence without explaining or making explicit what that is. Most importantly for our purposes, the principle doesn't explain why, if there is some essence to Black Sabbath's music, that essence cannot be captured or replicated by musicians other than the original members.

Of course, this is a matter of great controversy among Sabbath fans. As I mentioned at the beginning, some fans claim that the band continued to be Sabbath when Dio took over vocal duties for Ozzy, but ceased to be Sabbath once Dio left the band. Their rationale for this claim is often that the Dio-fronted era of Sabbath retained the essence of the original band, but that this essence was lost on those subsequent recordings on which neither Dio nor Ozzy sang. There are also those fans who discovered Black Sabbath during Dio's tenure and who regard *Heaven and Hell* and *Mob Rules* as the albums that forged and defined their connection to the band. Both groups of fans will simply reject the revised principle on the grounds that there is no reason to think that the Ozzy era is somehow more authentically Black Sabbath than the Dio era. We'll return to the question of Sabbath's musical essence in due course.

Pushing on, we might say that *Black Sabbath is primarily a legal entity. A band is Black Sabbath if and only if it records or tours under the lawful ownership of the name "Black Sabbath."* Call this the "legal interpretation" of Black Sabbath. This principle is often cited by those fans who espouse the most permissive interpretation of what constitutes the identity of Black Sabbath, according to which every line-up that toured and recorded as "Black Sabbath," even ones in which Tony Iommi was the sole remaining original member, counts as an authentic version of the band. Defenders of the "legal interpretation" point to the fact that in the mid-1980s the other original members transferred ownership of the Sabbath name to Tony Iommi. Since Iommi then owned the name, these fans say, those line-ups that toured and recorded under the name "Black Sabbath" during this time period are indeed later versions of the band.

One problem with this interpretation is that legal ownership can usually be transferred to just about anyone—including people who bear no relation at all to the history of Black Sabbath. Suppose— thought experiment alert!—that Justin Bieber purchased the rights to the name "Black Sabbath" and performed his hit "One Less Lonely Girl" under its banner. Would that count as a genuine iteration of the band? Almost every Black Sabbath fan who has ever lived would insist that it would not. When you press fans who subscribe to the legal interpretation on this issue, they usually point out that since Iommi was always the primary songwriter and unofficial bandleader,[5] he is the essence of Black Sabbath. Despite what these fans profess, it's just not true that they defer to legal authority in settling questions about Black Sabbath's identity. Instead, they just identify the essence of Black Sabbath's music with Iommi's guitar playing.

Thus what the fans who defend the "permissive" interpretation usually end up saying is something like this: *a band is Black Sabbath if and only if (1) Tony Iommi is in the band and (2) the band records or tours under the name "Black Sabbath."* But like before, a specter haunts our principle, and his name is Justin Bieber. For suppose that Tony Iommi gave up guitar to play the harp and let Justin Bieber join the band as both singer and songwriter. Would our permissive fans regard that band as Black Sabbath? Of course not. So the "permissive" fans really believe something like the following: *a band is Black Sabbath if and only if (1) Tony Iommi is in the band as the primary songwriter and guitar player and (2) the band records or tours under the name "Black Sabbath."* More than any other principle so far, this principle identifies Tony Iommi's songwriting contribution as what is essential about Black Sabbath.

Any Sabbath fan who is aware of Tony Iommi's unflagging determination to keep some version of the band going should have some sympathy for this principle.[6] However, while there might be much to be said for this principle, purists such as myself will respond that Bill Ward's jazz-inspired drumming, Geezer Butler's bass playing and lyrics, and Ozzy Osbourne's vocal delivery are all equally integral to the essence of the band. Likewise, Dio fans will point to his tenure in the band as a time of creative and artistic resurgence for Black Sabbath, as well as renewed interest from fans. Each Sabbath fan thus seems to have her own ideas about what constitutes the "real" Black Sabbath, and the thought experiments we've appealed to haven't been too helpful in deciding between them. It seems we've reached an impasse, with no party to the dispute willing to concede any ground. However, before we begin shouting "Sabbath, bloody Sabbath!" in anger, let's consider the possibility that we've been thinking about this problem in the wrong way.

Avoiding the Fictional Seduction of Bad Metaphysics

All along we've been assuming that there is some fact about Black Sabbath's identity that could, hopefully, be codified in a principle. Perhaps there is some determinate set of criteria that specifies the necessary and sufficient conditions of a band's being Black Sabbath, and I invite the reader who hasn't given up on such a project to propose principles and thought experiments for herself.[7] In the meantime, let's reconsider our assumption that there is a fact of the matter concerning which line-ups were "really" Black Sabbath.

Debates about Black Sabbath's identity usually—and usually very quickly—transform into debates about whether some era captures what those particular fans consider to be distinctively musically valuable. In truth, music resonates with us in highly personal ways, and we might express this in the thought that every Sabbath fan has her own "connection" to the music. For one person, that connection might begin and end with Iommi's riffs. For another, it might be Dio's operatic vocals on "Neon Knights." For me, it is that unique musical aura that only the original members were able to create. If you think the dark atmosphere of "Into the Void" or the proggy instrumentalism and existential dread of "Killing Yourself to Live" are emblematic examples of the "Sabbath Sound" you hold so dear, then Dio's power metal vocals and fascination with "dragons and kings" will seem off-putting.

Which brings me to why I am so reluctant to extend the Sabbath label beyond the Ozzy years. With all due respect to my fellow Sabbath fans, it is my contention that the post-Ozzy line-ups lack the sophistication and emotional depth of the original Sabbath Sound. To take just one example, consider "Hand of Doom," a song that communicates the horrors of a shell-shocked veteran's descent into addiction with eloquent intensity. Released at a time when vets were returning home from Vietnam, the song does not spare us in its candid portrayal of the psychological ravages of war. It begins with an isolated bass line as Ozzy delivers Geezer Butler's lyrics in a mocking, malevolent tone: "First it was the bomb / Vietnam, napalm / Disillusioning / You push the needle in." Thus establishing the sense of alienation and despair, the song crescendos into an urgent, pounding guitar riff, until finally giving way to the thump-thump-thump of Tony and Geezer's wall of sound: "You're having a good time, baby / But that won't last / Your mind's all full of things / You're living too fast / Go out, enjoy yourself / Don't bottle it in / You need someone to help you / Stick the needle in." The song ends as the original bass line slowly fades out, reminding the listener that there is no redemption awaiting our soldier, only death. This is deep, resonant music that touches on momentous themes with real artistry.

Some people who accept my general analysis—let's call them the "near purists"—feel that while Ozzy, Tony, and Geezer are essential, Bill Ward, being "just the drummer," can be replaced. As I write this, the proposed reunion tour of the original members of Black Sabbath is disintegrating, as Ward found the contract he was offered "unsign-able"[8] and the rest of the guys are planning to continue without him.[9] The powers-that-be are banking on the fact that most people would be just as content to see a partial reunion with a hired drummer as they would be to see the original four.

To the near purists, I suggest listening to the song "Black Sabbath," the very template for the Sabbath Sound. Pay attention to how Ward reacts to the interplay created by the tritone melody and Ozzy's sinister delivery. A light touch of the cymbal keeps the beat, but the drum fills are sparse, brooding, building sonic tension by straying just a bit off time, hanging back until a slow but emphatic roll brings them to the foreground. It is one of the most ominous pieces of drumming ever recorded, yet it never sounds overly assertive or self-indulgent, and most people wouldn't even notice it unless it were to go missing. Ward's preternatural feel gives the song a dimension—a heaviness, both musical and emotional—without which it wouldn't be nearly as dark and powerful. Ward's drumming is just as integral to the Sabbath Sound as Tony's riffs, Geezer's distorted rumble, and Ozzy's demonic whine.[10] Replace any of these guys, and you might have a great rock band—you just won't have Black Sabbath.

But while I don't think a partial reunion deserves the name "Black Sabbath," I also don't think that the above reflections are getting at any kind of deep metaphysical fact about the band's identity. Instead, what I think these reflections show is that such disagreements are really disagreements concerning a kind of aesthetic judgment. To my mind, the Ozzy era captured something distinctively aesthetically valuable, and it is that unique sound—that musical "essence," if you like—that I am referring to when I say that Black Sabbath is my favorite band.

In general, when we debate whether some line-up is really Black Sabbath, what we are really doing is allowing our aesthetic preferences to determine which line-up or line-ups the term "Black Sabbath" signifies. By doing this, we restrict the application of the term in such a way that what appears to be a debate over a kind of fact is really a debate over differing aesthetic values. If this is right, then questions like "Is it still Sabbath without Ozzy?" will admit of true and determinate answers only if there are objective facts about aesthetic value. For independent philosophical reasons, I do not think there are such facts—and consequently, no true answer to the question with which we began. Some might take this to mean that we should just stop debating the question, but I will continue to argue my case as if there were a definitive answer, because having this debate with my fellow Sabbath fans is just too much fun. And besides, no one can listen to "Hand of Doom" and deny that the real Sabs have always been Ozzy, Tony, Geezer, and Bill. Right?

Notes

1. www.black-sabbath.com/theband/.
2. Kant uses the metaphor of a "court of reason" (in German: *ein Gerichtshof der Vernunft*) in "Über das Mißlingen aller philosophischen Versuche in der Theodicee" (On the Failure of All Philosophical Attempts at Theodicy), 255, which can be found on-line at http://korpora.zim.uni-duisburg-essen.de/Kant/aa08/255.html.
3. Thomas Hobbes, *De Corpore* ("On the Body"), Part 2, 11.7. Found on-line at www.philosophy.leeds.ac.uk/GMR/hmp/texts/modern/hobbes/decorpore.
4. This is implicit in the fact that Black Sabbath's 1978 tour was billed as their tenth anniversary tour.
5. From Ozzy's autobiography: "Officially, we didn't have a band leader. Unofficially, we all knew it was Tony. He was the oldest, the tallest, the best fighter, the best-looking, the most experienced, and the most obviously talented .... We all knew that Tony belonged right up there with the likes of Clapton and Hendrix. Pound for pound, he could match any of them. He was our ticket to the big time." *I Am Ozzy* (New York: Grand Central Publishing, 2010), 69.
6. This is well documented in Iommi's autobiography *Iron Man: My Journey Through Heaven and Hell with Black Sabbath* (Cambridge, MA: Da Capo Press, 2011).
7. Once, while listening to the song "I" off the *Dehumanizer* album, and while subjecting myself to the kind of rigorous self-examination that inevitably accompanies such a listening experience, I reconsidered my purism and entertained the possibility that a band counts as Sabbath if and only if (1) both Tony Iommi and Geezer Butler are in the band as the guitar player and bassist, respectively, (2) Bill Ward was at least offered the opportunity to play drums, and (3) the band toured and wrote under the name "Black Sabbath." What do you think of this principle? Can you think of any thought experiments that might challenge it?
8. www.black-sabbath.com/2012/02/bill-ward-out-of-reunion-maybe/.

9. www.black-sabbath.com/2012/02/the-sabs-respond-to-bill/.

10. But don't take my word for it. Here's Tony Iommi comparing Bill Ward to Vinny Appice and other drummers who have tried to fill Ward's shoes: "There's quite a difference between the way Vinny and Bill play drums. Vinny came in with all these fast rolls, which Bill didn't play at all. Bill was from the John Bonham and Cozy Powell camp. He was good, but he had his own style, he created his unique thing. Very unorthodox. Bill wouldn't play a straightforward beat, he always put some little bits in, like a percussionist.... In playing with Vinny I had to retrain my mind as well. I thought, Christ, he's really good, but he cannot be too precise on the old songs, he's got to be a bit laid back. Black Sabbath was never exact on the timing. With Bill we would start off in one tempo and end up in another; it was a natural feel and Bill had that feel. I had to go through everything with Vinny, as I later have with every drummer, trying to coax him into playing the old songs as they were," *Iron Man*, 197–198.

Chapter 12

Fightin' Words
Sabbath Doesn't Need the Ozzman

Wesley D. Cray

Like other longtime metalheads, I've had the debate many times: is it still Sabbath without Ozzy? Despite the name "Black Sabbath" appearing on releases featuring Ronnie James Dio, Ian Gillan, Glenn Hughes, Ray Gillen, and Tony Martin, many fans will argue that it just isn't really Sabbath without the Ozzman himself handling the mic. And this, of course, is to focus on just the vocal element of the band, ignoring similar questions pertaining to the long line of bassists and drummers who have filled the spots often left vacant by the classic rhythm section of Geezer Butler and Bill Ward. But when it comes down to philosophical analysis, are any of the Ozz-less line-ups that called themselves "Black Sabbath" *really* Black Sabbath? Some of them are, I say, and some of them aren't.

Bands vs Line-Ups

Philosophers throughout history have engaged in the study of metaphysics—loosely, the study of reality, of *what there is* and *what it's like*. Metaphysicians ask questions about what exists, what properties things have, and how things relate to one another. They also like distinctions. René Descartes (1596–1650), for example, championed a metaphysical distinction between *mental substance* and *physical substance*,[1] and many others have drawn metaphysical

Black Sabbath and Philosophy: Mastering Reality, First Edition. Edited by William Irwin.
© 2013 John Wiley & Sons, Inc. Published 2013 by John Wiley & Sons, Inc.

distinctions between so-called *concrete* objects (things like chairs, donkeys, and electrons) and so-called *abstract* objects (things like numbers).[2]

We can draw a metaphysical distinction here, as well: there are *bands* and then there are *line-ups*. A *line-up* is an ensemble of particular musicians. Tony Iommi, Geezer Butler, Bill Ward, and Ozzy Osbourne together compose one particular line-up, while Tony Iommi, Geezer Butler, Vinny Appice, and Ronnie James Dio compose another. Line-ups are fragile, in the sense that any change in membership will result in a change in line-up. We can think of line-ups like married couples: swap out one husband for another, and you have a new couple.

Bands, though, can survive changes in members. It would be silly, after all, to say that Pink Floyd ended when David Gilmour joined in with Syd Barrett, Roger Waters, Nick Mason, and Richard Wright in 1967. Since bands *can* survive changes in members and line-ups *can't*, it follows that bands are distinct from line-ups. Armed with this metaphysical distinction, we can now state what it is for a band to survive a line-up change: a band survives a line-up change if and only if that band is identified with one line-up at *time 1* and with another line-up at a later *time 2*. But this raises another metaphysical question: what is it for a line-up at a *time 1* and a line-up at a later *time 2* to both be the same band?

A Sabbath By Any Other Name Would Be as Black

To be clear, this isn't an issue about band *names*. Consider the distinction between the name "Tony Iommi" and the person Tony Iommi. It's important to recognize that the two are quite different. We don't want to go around saying of the name that it writes awesome guitar riffs, or of the person that he begins with the letter T.[3] Along the same lines, if we want to make progress, we need to keep the name "Black Sabbath" distinct from the band Black Sabbath.

It can't be that all it takes for a line-up to be a particular band is for that line-up to call itself by that band's name. If that were the case, then you and I could form a line-up, call ourselves "Black Sabbath," and really *be* Black Sabbath. Similarly, the 2006 line-up of the Seattle-based drone act Earth would be the same band as the 1968

Iommi-Butler-Ward-Osbourne line-up, who also called themselves "Earth." Insofar as we think that you and I can't just decide to be Black Sabbath, and that the 2006 Earth is a different band than that early incarnation of Sabbath, we should reject the claim that sameness of name is all it takes for sameness of band.

So sameness of name isn't all it takes for sameness of band, but is it still required? It seems not, or else we wouldn't be able to make sense of the intuition that bands can change their names. As just mentioned, a band formerly known as "Earth" changed its name to "Black Sabbath," just as "Rhapsody" and "The New Yardbirds" changed their names to "Rhapsody of Fire" and "Led Zeppelin," respectively. Sameness of name, then, is neither necessary nor sufficient for sameness of band. This seems right—after all, our question isn't about which line-ups are *called* "Black Sabbath." To answer that, we could just check some liner notes. Instead, we want to know which line-ups really *are* Black Sabbath, and that question is much more difficult.

Going Through Changes

We want an account of the metaphysics of band identity over time, or, more specifically, of band identity through changes in line-up. So we need to know what it is for a line-up at a *time 1* and a line-up at a later *time 2* to really *be* the same band. To be acceptable, any potential answer needs to be at least (i) metaphysically coherent, (ii) consistent with most of our intuitions about the matter, and (iii) general enough to apply to any band, not just Black Sabbath.

Metaphysical coherence is really a minimum standard. Good metaphysics, after all, should not come with contradictions or incoherence. If, for example, an account of the metaphysics of band identity over time tells us that the 1981 line-up of Iommi-Butler-Dio-Appice both *is* and *isn't* Black Sabbath, we have good reason to reject that account.

We require consistency with most of our intuitions because, when it comes down to it, those intuitions are our starting points—they're the data. As such, we should reject any account that tells us that, say, Ozzy's membership alone is all it takes for a given line-up to be Black Sabbath, since such an account would tell us that the line-up that recorded *Blizzard of Ozz* (1980)—Randy Rhoads, Bob Daisley, Lee

Kerslake, and the Ozzman himself[4]—was really Black Sabbath, and our intuitions tell us that that's clearly false.

Finally, to avoid getting led astray by various details of any particular band, a good account should be general enough to apply to all bands. After all, if we were to build our account by looking at Sabbath alone, we might be tempted to conclude that a line-up at a *time 1* and a line-up at a later *time 2* are the same band if and only if they share the same guitarist. But it's clear that there are bands that have survived guitarist changes in their line-ups: Iron Maiden, Judas Priest, Megadeth, and Metallica, to name a few. We need our account to make sense of that issue, too.

Criteria, Bloody Criteria

What criteria must be satisfied in order for a line-up at *time 1* and a line-up at a later *time 2* to be the same band? For starters, the successive line-ups must have some overlap. Think of how odd it would be if Tony, Geezer, Bill, and Ozzy got together and put out an album under the name "Led Zeppelin." Remember that sameness of name isn't sufficient for sameness of band. So sure, such an album might have been recorded by a band *calling itself* "Led Zeppelin," but intuition clearly tells us that the album was not recorded by Led Zeppelin themselves. For two successive line-ups to really be the same band, they must share some members; call this the *continuity criterion*.

How many members must the successive line-ups share? If we accept that the album *Scum* (1987) was recorded by just one band—Napalm Death—despite the two halves of the record having been recorded by line-ups that share only one member—Mick Harris—we should say that the amount of continuity required is just that: one member. Further support for this minimal take on the requirement can be found in the intuition that the ritualistic bass-driven duo Om was still the same band after Chris Hakius was replaced by Emil Eros in 2008. It would not be hard at all to find many more examples. So, to satisfy the continuity criterion, successive line-ups must share at least one member.

What about non-successive line-ups? They can satisfy the continuity criterion, too. If, for example, line-up *a* and line-up *c* share no members, they still satisfy the continuity criterion as long as there is a line-up *b* that came directly after and shares members with *a*, and comes directly before and shares members with *c*. In other words, if we can form a chain of line-ups such that each line-up shares a member with the line-ups directly before and after it, we can say that the line-ups at the beginning and end of the chain satisfy the continuity criterion, even if there are no members that run the length of the chain.

Of course, the continuity criterion won't be enough. The line-up that recorded *Never Say Die!* (1978) shares a member with the line-up that recorded *Blizzard of Ozz*, but again, intuition clearly tells us that Ozzy's early solo band is not Black Sabbath. Satisfying the continuity criterion, then, will be required for band identity over time, but that's not all it takes. To have a full account of the metaphysics of the matter, we're going to need something more—we also need to look at the *intentions* of the line-up. Now, intending to be a band cannot be all it takes to be that band, or else you and I could get together whenever we wanted and be Black Sabbath just by intending to be Black Sabbath. Not only is this intuitively unacceptable, but it also violates the continuity criterion—assuming that you, the reader, weren't a member of the latest of Sabbath's many incarnations.

Such intentions do seem to be necessary, however, though it will take some spelling out to see why. First, we ask what it is for a line-up to intend to be a particular band. It doesn't seem that the line-up of Tony, Geezer, Bill, and Ozzy had to actively think to themselves "we intend to be Black Sabbath!" in order to intend to be Black Sabbath. Consider my actions as I am writing this chapter. It doesn't seem that I have to actively think to myself "I intend to finish this sentence" in order to intend to finish this sentence. The intention is something I have, whether I notice it or not. How can we detect such intentions? Well, we can start by noting behavior. I typed, thought about word choice, revised once or twice; in other words, I directly engaged in behavior that led to me finishing that sentence. Noting this behavior puts you in a good position to guess my intentions. So, to see if, at any given time, Tony and the others intend to be Black Sabbath, we run the same sort of test. In other words, we look to see if they are engaging in behavior that indicates an intention to be Black Sabbath. If so, we can conclude that they have such an intention.

What sorts of behaviors might tip us off? The answer is simple: the use of certain musical styles, lyrical imagery, album artwork, and personas, for starters, as well as the adoption of the band name itself.

Is the line-up writing heavy riffs and scorching solos, penning lyrics with dark and macabre subject matter, adorning their albums with images of crosses and devils, and calling themselves "Black Sabbath"? If so, it's probably safe to bet that they are intending to be Black Sabbath. Of course, none of these behaviors are necessary, as Sabbath did occasionally eschew heavy riffs, dark lyrics, their typical imagery, and, as I'll argue later, perhaps even their usual name. The method also isn't fool-proof, as it's conceivable that they could behave as they have without really having the relevant intentions. But, in general, the presence of such behavior is a pretty good guide to the line-up's intentions.

We now have a method for forming educated guesses about a line-up's intentions, but why think that intending to be a particular band is *necessary* for being that band? Well, if it weren't, we'd have cases in which a line-up is a particular band by accident. If a line-up could be a particular band without intending to be so, then, at any given time, whether or not they are intending to be Sabbath, Tony and company could have really been some other band entirely! That would be a very strange and undesirable result, and the desire to avoid it forms the motivation for accepting what we can call the *intention criterion*: a line-up at *time 1* and a line-up at a later *time 2* are the same band only if both line-ups intend to be that band.

Is the satisfaction of both the continuity and intention criteria all it takes for sameness of band? No, and we can see why by considering the Norwegian black metal band Gorgoroth. The early 2007 Gorgoroth line-up included Infernus, King ov Hell, and Gaahl.[5] King ov Hell and Gaahl attempted to fire Infernus, prompting Infernus to take his former band mates to court in an attempt to retain control of the band. In the meantime, both parties rounded out their respective line-ups, called themselves "Gorgoroth," and carried on with similar aesthetics. But the question remained: which band was *really* Gorgoroth? Both line-ups satisfied the continuity and intention criteria, but it can't be that both line-ups were really Gorgoroth. Such a conclusion would violate our requirement of metaphysical coherence, as it would tell us that the Gorgoroth of early 2007 was the same band as both of the later "Gorgoroths." Intuition tells us that those are *two distinct bands*—if you saw both Infernus's line-up and King ov Hell and Gaahl's line-up perform on the same night, you would say that you saw *two* bands that night, not just *one*. So to avoid incoherent conclusions, we require that, at any given time, any given band should correspond to at most one line-up.[6] Call this the *uniqueness criterion*: a line-up at a *time 1* and a line-up at a later *time 2* are the same band only if no other line-up at either time is that band.

We now have our account of the metaphysics of band identity over time: a line-up at a *time 1* and a line-up at a later *time 2* are the same band if and only if they satisfy the continuity, intention, and uniqueness criteria. This account meets our requirements of metaphysical coherence, sensitivity to intuition, and generality. So are we done? Are we in a position to decide whether it's still Sabbath without Ozzy? No, not yet—there's one more complication to address.

How Essential Is the Ozzman?

Suppose that, back in 1979, when the other band members agreed to fire Ozzy from the band, Bill, his best friend in the band at the time, decided to quit and go with him. Suppose further that Tony and Geezer found a new drummer and vocalist and intended to continue on as Black Sabbath, and that Ozzy and Bill got together with a new guitarist and bassist and also intended to continue on as Black Sabbath. Both line-ups satisfy the continuity and intention criteria, but it can't be that both satisfy the uniqueness criterion—they can't *both* be Black Sabbath. In order to break the tie and determine which line-up would really be Black Sabbath, we need to look at the notion of *essential members*.[7]

Common sense tells us that not all band members are equal. If Billy Corgan quit the Smashing Pumpkins, the Pumpkins would be no more. Nirvana died when Kurt Cobain died, and it would simply make no sense to talk about the Melvins without King Buzzo. This is because these members are *essential*—if they go, the band goes. Not all members of all bands are essential, of course, or else line-up changes would be impossible. When Chad Channing left Nirvana, for instance, the band carried on. But when an *essential* member of a band departs, the band is done, as no line-up without that member can really be that band.[8]

Of the members of Black Sabbath, the one that is most obviously essential is Tony Iommi—the founder, leader, chief songwriter, and creative backbone of the band. I take it to be uncontroversial that, without Tony, there would be no Sabbath. Imagine Tony departing and the line-up continuing with the intention to be Black Sabbath— this would be even more absurd than thinking that Martin Eric Ain and Franco Sesa could seriously intend to carry on as Celtic Frost after Tom Gabriel Fischer left the band in 2008! This would be akin to me intending to finish typing my earlier sentence despite the fact that my keyboard is missing—or, more accurately, despite the fact that my body had been obliterated.

But what about Ozzy? Is *he* an essential member of Black Sabbath? If so, then, just as with Tony, any Ozz-less line-up can't be Black Sabbath, even if they call themselves by that name, play in that style, adopt that imagery, and so on. The range of albums from *Heaven and Hell* (1980) all the way through *Forbidden* (1995) wouldn't really be Sabbath albums after all, despite what it says in the liner notes and on the album artwork—even despite what the band members themselves might say. But if Ozzy is *not* an essential member, the place for those albums in the Sabbath discography might be saved. What needs to be settled, then, is whether Ozzy is essential.

The notion of essentiality is hard to pin down, but, as alluded to a moment ago, we can make some headway by returning to the intention criterion: a line-up is a particular band only if that line-up intends to be that band. Not all line-ups operate as completely egalitarian democracies, with each member doing an equal part of the intention-forming.[9] Consider the Swedish progressive metal band Opeth. Martin Axenrot does not appear to have much control in the band at all, so he's not an essential member. Mikael Åkerfeldt, however, calls the shots—he writes the majority of the music, pens the lyrics, determines the band's visual component—making him an essential member.[10] Put another way, Axenrot doesn't play any substantial role in directing the line-up's intentions *to be Opeth*, whereas Åkerfeldt clearly does. It is for similar reasons that Tony is clearly an essential member of Sabbath, just as Billy Corgan, Kurt Cobain, King Buzzo, and Tom Gabriel Fischer are essential members of their respective bands: these folks all play substantial roles in directing their line-ups' intentions to be their respective bands.[11]

Notice that essentiality comes in degrees. Geezer had more intention-directing control than Bill,[12] so Geezer is more essential than Bill, who is probably not essential at all.[13] But if essentiality comes in degrees, what happens when a *sort-of-essential* member, like

Geezer, departs? We don't want to say that a Geezer-less line-up that meets the continuity and uniqueness criteria only *sort of* meets the intention criterion and hence is really only *sort of* Black Sabbath. That would be to say that the relation between the line-up and the band only *sort of* holds, which is metaphysically incoherent. Maybe we should say instead that, even though no Geezer-less line-up really *is* Sabbath, some of them stand in some other mysterious relation—the *sort-of-is* relation, perhaps—with the band. But it's not clear that that's any better.

These issues are hard, but thankfully, we can avoid them. After all, they would burden us only if Ozzy were an essential—or even sort-of-essential—member of Black Sabbath, which he's not. That's right, I said it: *Ozzy is not an essential—or even sort-of-essential—member of Black Sabbath*. It's well known that Tony wrote nearly all of the music and that Geezer wrote most of the lyrics (at least in the early days). Tony came up with the sound, and the band's trademark eponymous song was inspired by one of Geezer's dreams. And even though Ozzy did write the vocal melodies, they would often, as Tony himself put it, "follow the riff."[14] Ozzy might have been the public face of the band from 1970 through 1978, but he was never enough of a contributor to make him an essential member. He just didn't play enough of an intention-directing role.

To some, these are fightin' words, but that doesn't make them any less true. For further support of the claim that Ozzy is not essential, recall reading earlier in this chapter that Ozzy was fired from the band in 1979. I imagine that you read that sentence without giving it a second thought. If Ozzy was really an essential member, the sentence "Ozzy was fired from Black Sabbath" would make no sense—but it clearly does. If, however, you were to read that *Tony* was fired from the band, you probably would stop and scratch your head. This is because, unlike Ozzy, Tony is essential.

Which "Sabbath" Is Really Sabbath?

So is it still Sabbath without Ozzy? I say yes—most of the time. Given the metaphysics just laid out, there are several Ozzy-less incarnations of Black Sabbath. The line-ups that recorded *Heaven and Hell, Mob Rules* (1981), *Born Again* (1983), *Seventh Star* (1986), *The Eternal*

Idol (1987), *Headless Cross* (1989), *TYR* (1990), *Dehumanizer* (1992), *Cross Purposes* (1994), and *Forbidden* (1995) all satisfy the continuity criterion, with at least Tony appearing on each album.[15] They all satisfy the uniqueness criterion, as well.

Not all of those line-ups satisfy the intention criterion, however. *Seventh Star* was not intended to be a Sabbath album, but was put out under that name (actually, under the name "Black Sabbath featuring Tony Iommi") due to a decision made by the record label. Similar reports have been made about *Born Again*.[16] Regarding *Cross Purposes*, Geezer has said that "[it] wasn't even supposed to be a Sabbath album," that "it was like an Iommi/Butler project album."[17] This all gives us good reason to believe that the line-ups behind *Seventh Star*, *Born Again*, and *Cross Purposes* failed to satisfy the intention criterion, and hence, weren't really Black Sabbath.[18]

What about Heaven and Hell, the Iommi-Butler-Dio-Appice super group that formed in 2006 and released *The Devil You Know* in 2009? When it comes to being Sabbath, that line-up meets both the continuity and uniqueness criteria, but does it meet the intention criterion? Perhaps so. Iommi's characteristic riffs and Butler's familiar bass lines were there, as was the band's imagery—notice not just the title of the album, but also the little devil on the cover! And just a year prior, that same line-up had recorded three new songs under the name "Black Sabbath" to be released on the compilation *Black Sabbath: The Dio Years* (2007). This is all evidence—not conclusive evidence, mind you, but evidence nonetheless—that the line-up really did intend to be Black Sabbath, but for perhaps legal or political or personal reasons, refrained from using the name.[19] And while the band did not play any material from Dio-less albums, it did draw the vast majority of its live set from canonical Sabbath albums, namely *Heaven and Hell*, *Mob Rules*, and *Dehumanizer*. So there is a case to be made that the 2006–2010 Iommi-Butler-Dio-Appice line-up meets the criteria required for being Black Sabbath. If so, the band called "Heaven and Hell" was just Sabbath going by a different name.[20]

What about the Geezer-less *The Eternal Idol*, *Headless Cross*, *TYR*, and *Forbidden*? The line-ups that recorded these albums satisfy the continuity and uniqueness criteria, but whether or not they satisfy the intention criterion depends on what we say about Geezer and sort-of-essential members. If he's really fully essential, then his absence results in a failure to satisfy the intention criterion, so none of those albums are really Sabbath albums. If he's not essential, then the intention criterion can be satisfied, so those albums are in the clear. What if, as suggested earlier, he's only a sort-of-essential member? Are they only *sort of* Sabbath albums? Again, this is a very difficult topic, and one that's not directly relevant to the Ozzy issue, so we'll leave it to the side for now. That's one of the great things about philosophy—there's always more left to do!

While Ozzy most definitely was a big part of Black Sabbath's history and legacy, by looking at the metaphysics of band identity over time we see that his absence doesn't preclude certain subsequent line-ups from rightfully and truly claiming to *be* Black Sabbath. It *is* still Sabbath without Ozzy—*sometimes*.[21]

Notes

1. For the classic arguments in favor of such a distinction, see René Descartes, *Meditations on the First Philosophy*, trans. J. Cottingham (Cambridge: Cambridge University Press, 1996).

2. For a nice discussion of the distinction between abstract objects and concrete objects, including a discussion of whether such a distinction ultimately makes sense, see David Lewis, *On the Plurality of Worlds* (Malden, MA: Blackwell, 1986), 81–86.

3. This is to touch on the distinction between *using* an expression and *mentioning* the expression. On this distinction, the influential twentieth-century philosopher Willard Van Orman Quine writes: "To mention Boston we use 'Boston' or a synonym, and to mention 'Boston' we use ' 'Boston' ' or a synonym. ' 'Boston' ' contains six letters and just one pair of quotation marks; 'Boston' contains six letters and no quotation marks; and Boston contains some 800,000 people," *Mathematical Logic, Revised Edition* (Cambridge, MA: Harvard University Press, 1981), 24.

4. As well as perhaps Don Airey, though his status as a band member is debatable. There are interesting questions to be raised about the metaphysical relationships between line-ups and session members—what deep difference is there between a *real* member and a mere *session* member, after all? Geoff Nicholls's status as a member of Sabbath on some albums is an interesting issue in this regard. But, unfortunately, we won't have the space to address such questions here.

5. There was no official drummer in this line-up, though Frost played session drums on the 2006 album *Ad Majorem Sathanas Gloriam*.

6. We need not require, though, that any given line-up correspond to at most one band at a time. It seems that you and I alone could get together and form several different bands at the same time, after all.

7. This is essentially (no pun intended) how the Oslo City District Court decided the aforementioned Gorgoroth case, leading to the decision that Infernus's line-up was really Gorgoroth. Technically, the decision was that Infernus won the rights to the band's *name*, but it's clear that the band's identity was really what was at stake.

8. It is for this reason that many fans of the Norwegian black metal band Mayhem refuse to consider any line-up without Euronymous, a purportedly essential member, to really be Mayhem. One could take the debate over whether later line-ups going by the name "Mayhem" really *are* Mayhem to amount to the debate over whether Euronymous was an essential member after all. Given what has been said so far, it seems very plausible to say that he is. This would imply that, according to the metaphysics on offer in this chapter, it might be that the only studio album Mayhem ever really put out was *De Mysteriis Dom Sathanas* (1994)!

9. Though some are. In such cases, it seems that each member would be *equally* essential, meaning that the band becomes as fragile as the line-up. Joy Division might be a relevant example, as the four members all agreed to abandon the "Joy Division" name if any member left, indicating perhaps that they no longer intended to perform as that band. This pact led to Joy Division's break-up after the death of Ian Curtis in 1980, and the subsequent forming of New Order by the remaining members of the Joy Division line-up.

10. Interestingly enough, Åkerfeldt was not an original member of Opeth, which means that there are some cases in which a member is essential without being an original member. It looks like members can *become* essential, then, by taking over more of the duty of directing the line-up's intentions. Perhaps we can also say that essential members, as they relinquish control, can become *inessential*, so that if they leave, whether or not the band survives depends on whether they were essential or inessential at the time of their departure.

11. Our intuitions might get a bit shaky when purportedly essential members die. After all, if Steve Harris passed away, couldn't Iron Maiden continue to tour? Perhaps so, but this might indicate to us that Harris is not as essential to Maiden as we might initially think. King Buzzo is clearly an essential member of the Melvins, as is Billy Corgan with respect to the Smashing Pumpkins; if either passed away, those bands would certainly cease to be. Likewise, it would be absurd to think of Nirvana reforming without Kurt Cobain, or of Dio (the band) reuniting

without Dio (the person). Perhaps, then, we can use this as a test for the essentiality of a member: if a member were to die and intuition tells us that the band could nevertheless continue, that member is not essential. I do not intend to endorse this test here, though I find it to be plausible. Notice, though, that if it is accepted, and we think that Iron Maiden could continue to tour without Steve Harris, we would have to conclude that Harris is not really an essential member of the band.

12. Insofar as Geezer wrote many of the band's lyrics.

13. In fact, as of the time of this writing, the status of the long-awaited Sabbath reunion seems to be that Ozzy, Tony, and Geezer intend on being Black Sabbath whether Bill (who is currently opting out due to contractual reasons) participates or not.

14. Steven Rosen, *The Story of Black Sabbath: Wheels of Confusion* (Chessington, Surrey: Castle Communications, 1996), 98. Of course, Tony's comment might exaggerate how often Ozzy actually relied on this technique, but it also sheds light on his attitude toward Ozzy's contributions at the time. As the only clearly essential member of the band, his attitude toward the others in the band is particularly relevant here.

15. To keep things tidy, I restrict the discussion to just studio albums.

16. Dave Thompson, *Smoke on the Water: The Deep Purple Story* (Toronto: ECW Press, 2004), 233–239.

17. Rosen, 130.

18. In Martin Popoff's *Black Sabbath FAQ: All That's Left to Know on the First Name in Metal* (Milwaukee: Backbeat Books, 2011), Geezer is cited as saying that, despite his wanting to continue under a different name, the record label made the band continue under the name "Black Sabbath." It is not clear, however, whether Geezer's desire was to rename the band or to be a new band entirely. Looking at Dave Ling's liner notes for the 2008 re-issue of *Heaven and Hell*, however, we see that it was clearly Tony's intent to carry on as the *same* band: "No matter how bad things got, I didn't even consider giving up," Tony said. He goes on to say that he "believed in the band" and asks "what would be the point of breaking it up just to go away and form another?" This statement indicates that Tony—the member with the most intention-directing power—saw the *Heaven and Hell* line-up as the same band as the one that recorded the previous albums.

19. The band members themselves can't seem to agree what the reasons for the name change were. See Popoff, *Black Sabbath FAQ*, 298–299.

20. Further support of this claim comes from Tony's comments in the liner notes of Heaven and Hell's 2007 release *Live from Radio City Music Hall*, where he talks about "going out under the *name* Heaven & Hell instead of Black Sabbath" (my emphasis), but gives no indication that

he thinks of the group as a new *band*. Remember, difference in name is not sufficient for difference in band, even if the use of a certain name is sometimes *one* piece of evidence regarding the line-up's intentions. There is even evidence that Dio thought of the band as the same band as before, as indicated by his comments in the re-issued *Heaven and Hell*'s liner notes: "We're setting out on this for one more time, to reaffirm our legacy. No matter what anybody says or writes about us, we will always be friends—*getting back together three times* proves that. A *band* this good was simply meant to be" (my emphasis).

21. Many thanks to everyone who read and commented on this chapter, and to everyone I've had this argument with throughout the years. Special thanks to William Irwin, Ben Caplan, and Sabine Pelton. This chapter is dedicated to the ultimate heavy metal hero, Ronnie James Dio (1942–2010).

Chapter 13

The Name Remains the Same–But Should It?

Mark D. White

Each fan has his or her favorite member of Black Sabbath, without whom it *just isn't* Sabbath. Some fans can't imagine the band without the unique vocal delivery of Ozzy Osbourne, for others it's the thundering yet nimble bass lines of Geezer Butler, and for still others it's the jazz-inflected drumming of Bill Ward. Some fans will only listen to the original line-up, while others are fine with three or even just two of the founding members. But when it gets down to just one—guitarist Tony Iommi, the constant presence in every line-up of Black Sabbath—things can get dodgy, and fans can easily get frustrated. No matter how much they worship Tony, with his massive riffs and inventive solos, and even if they regard him as the musical core of Black Sabbath, some fans feel it's not alright for him to play under the name Black Sabbath without any of the other musicians who were there from the beginning.

The two previous chapters have debated the metaphysics of whether Sabbath can remain the same band through changes in line-ups. This chapter will focus on ethics. We'll look at the reasons fans have to expect a classic band like Sabbath to maintain a steady line-up—and any ethical obligations that bands have to do this—especially when the band keeps using the same name and reaping the goodwill that comes with it.

Black Sabbath and Philosophy: Mastering Reality, First Edition. Edited by William Irwin.
© 2013 John Wiley & Sons, Inc. Published 2013 by John Wiley & Sons, Inc.

On This Album, the Role of the Singer
Will Be Played By …

Those of us who listen to hard rock and metal bands from the 1970s and 1980s are all too familiar with line-up changes—so much so that fans automatically ask upon the release of a new album, "who's singing on *this* one?" For every band like Led Zeppelin that calls it quits after a founding member dies (or leaves), we have many more bands like Deep Purple, which has had 13 members since 1968.[1] For most fans, a change in singer is the most noticeable change, such as when Bruce Dickinson and Rob Halford left Iron Maiden and Judas Priest in the early nineties—both to return at the end of the decade. But other changes can make a big impact as well. Even the most casual fans noticed when guitarists Ritchie Blackmore and Michael Schenker left Deep Purple and UFO. Their replacements may have been very good, but the sound was not the same.

Through many changes, however, one thing usually remains the same: the name of the band. We could be cynical and assume that the motivation for this is purely commercial, coming from the band, managers, and (most often) record labels. But given the gradual ways in which line-ups change, continuity of the band's name is natural. If all but one member stick with the band, playing the music they helped write and make famous, why should the band's name change after one person leaves? But over time, enough musicians may leave to make the band unrecognizable from a decade before.

Although it may seem reasonable to keep the name when members are replaced, it does pose an ethical problem. A band's name is its calling card, its trademark, which appears on all of its albums, tour brochures, and so on. Often there's a slick logo or font to go with it, especially for metal bands; even nonmetal fans can easily recognize the classic logos of Iron Maiden and Metallica.[2] And when fans see the name—especially the large majority of fans who don't religiously follow everything that goes on with the band on their website or Facebook page—they expect to see a certain line-up playing their favorite songs. They want to see Sabbath with Ozzy singing "Iron Man," Purple with Ian Gillan singing "Smoke on the Water," and so forth. And when they see some newbie on stage singing or playing guitar, they feel ripped off, misled, and betrayed. Even the diehard fans, those who are in the know, often feel this way; they may not be surprised when Michael Schenker doesn't appear at a UFO show, but they may be resentful about it nonetheless.

I Saw It, I Saw It, I Tell You No Lies

But do they have a right to be resentful? Certainly they don't have a legal complaint; they bought an album or a ticket to see Black Sabbath, and they're hearing or seeing the line-up currently using that name. They're probably also hearing many of the songs they expected to hear, just not by all of the people they expected to hear performing them. It's much like seeing a TV show or movie where one of the actors is replaced by another in the same role. Same storyline, same writers, same character—different face. James Bond fans may be disappointed when a new actor takes over the role, but the movies (and the books) are based on the character, not the actor portraying him in any particular film.

So, do bands have an obligation or *duty* to give fans the line-up they want? The philosopher most closely associated with duty is Immanuel Kant (1724–1804), who derived duties from the *categorical imperative*, his formalization of the "moral law." The categorical imperative is used to judge *maxims*, or plans of action, to see if they're consistent with morality. In this case, Sabbath's maxim could have been "we will change band members without changing our band's name." If the categorical imperative rejects this maxim as immoral, that means there is a duty not to change band members without changing the band's name. This duty, in turn, would imply a right on the part of fans to have stable band line-ups as long as the name stays the same.

The most widely known version of the categorical imperative is called the Formula of Universal Law. It says that one should "act only according to that maxim whereby you can at the same time will that it should become a universal law."[3] This formula is based on Kant's position that all persons have an equal moral worth, or *dignity*, based on their capacity for independent choice, or *autonomy*. Therefore, if a person considers doing anything, that person must allow that everyone else must be able to do it also. If there would be an inconsistency or contradiction in everyone taking the action, then the action is forbidden. For example, lying is considered wrong because if everyone lied, no one would believe anybody, and lies would be self-defeating—and thus we have a duty not to lie.

Does this formula rule out our maxim of changing band members while keeping the same band name? No. If one band wants to do this, we must allow that every band can do this, which doesn't result in any contradiction. All bands *can* do this—and lots do, whenever they want, whether other bands do it or not. Fans may not like it, and it may hurt the bands' interests in the end, but as far as this formula of the categorical imperative is concerned, there's no ethical problem.[4]

Treating People Just Like Pawns in Chess

Another version of the categorical imperative, with a distinctly different feel and emphasis, is the Formula of Respect: "act in such a way that you treat humanity, whether in your own person or in the person of another, always at the same time as an end and never simply as a means."[5] This version is based on dignity and the equal moral status of all persons, as was the Formula of Universal Law, but the Formula of Respect requires that we treat each other (and ourselves) with ... well, respect. The idea is that we should not use people for our own purposes without treating them as equals at the same time. So lying is clearly prohibited. When we lie to someone to get something from them we use them as a tool or a "pawn." We do not respect him or her as a person with dignity and autonomy. You also abuse your own good name and reputation when you lie, which is using yourself merely as a means to your end.

How does our maxim of changing band members while keeping the same band name fare with this formula? Changing band members while keeping the same name makes some fans unhappy, to be sure, but does this amount to using them as mere means without at the same time considering them as ends? The concept of "using people" is vague. We make use of other people all the time, after all, especially in commerce. So when is it done wrongfully, or without treating them with respect?

Kant highlighted two ways you can use someone merely as means: coercion and deceit. The problem with each is consent. In cases of coercion the other person is denied the ability to consent to what you're doing, and in cases of deceit you're making consent impossible by concealing your true actions or motivations. In both cases, you are using the other person as a tool in your schemes—and if you have to use force or lie to a person to get his or her "cooperation," there's probably something wrong with what you're doing anyway![6]

So, do we have coercion or deceit in the case of bands changing members and not changing their names? The bands aren't forcing fans to buy the albums or attend the shows, so coercion doesn't apply. Deceit may exist, however, if the fans aren't aware of the line-up change, or are actually led to believe that members are present that actually aren't. Fans excited about the reunion of the original Sabbath line-up announced in November 2011 were understandably upset when Bill Ward announced in early 2012 that he wouldn't be participating. This was big news in the Sabbath and metal communities, but more casual fans may not be aware that when they buy the new Sabbath album or attend one of the shows, that they won't be seeing the entire original foursome.[7] They may feel cheated or tricked because it's called Black Sabbath and was billed (originally) as the founding members.

No Stranger to Record Companies

Sometimes the artists share our ethical concerns, not only in support of the fans but also in terms of the integrity of their own work. Take the *Seventh Star* album, for instance, which was billed as "Black Sabbath featuring Tony Iommi," even though Iommi's original plan was to record a solo album. Up to that point he had recorded 11 Black Sabbath studio albums, with three different singers, yet all of them featuring Geezer on bass and all but one with Bill on drums. But in 1985, after the dissolution of the *Born Again* line-up with Ian Gillan, Tony found himself alone, and, as he says, "without a band, I got the idea of doing a solo album with all different singers."[8]

Although he eventually recorded the entire *Seventh Star* album with Glenn Hughes—ironically, one of the musicians who joined Deep Purple after Ian Gillan's first departure from that band—record company pressures forced its release under the Black Sabbath name, which Tony was not happy about:

It was supposed to be a solo album. I certainly didn't want to release it as a Black Sabbath album, because I hadn't written it as a Black Sabbath album. I wanted the freedom for it to sound as it did and tour without calling the band Black Sabbath ... In the end [the album] was billed as "Black Sabbath featuring Tony Iommi." Neither I nor Glenn was pleased with it, because we felt we weren't doing the record justice presenting it this way. And to go out and play "War Pigs" and "Iron Man"—it just wasn't right.[9]

Indeed, the subsequent tour, which began with Glenn on vocals but finished with the late Ray Gillen, was billed simply as Black Sabbath—with Iommi the only holdover from previous line-ups—and they did play "War Pigs" and "Iron Man."

We can't be sure what Tony meant when he said "it just wasn't right," but there are several aspects of this situation he may have been referring to. One, as we mentioned earlier, was the element of deception to the fans. It was bad enough that an album that was never intended to be a Black Sabbath album was sold as such, but some fans attended the concerts expecting to see Tony playing with other musicians who had been in Sabbath previously (other than keyboardist Geoff Nicholls, who was rarely featured prominently on stage).

More personal to Tony, we can presume, was maintaining the integrity of the music itself. He hadn't meant to write a Black Sabbath album when he wrote *Seventh Star*. Billing it as Black Sabbath after the fact was a disservice to that album, which deserved to be judged as what it was, a Tony Iommi solo album (or an Iommi/Hughes joint project like 2005's *Fused*). It also casts a different light on the Black Sabbath name, which Tony had done so much to develop over the previous decade and a half.[10] Whatever one may think of *Seventh Star*, it is not, for most fans, a true Sabbath album, despite how the record company chose to label it.

Similar concerns were behind the billing of the band as Heaven & Hell for an album and tours, which saw the *Mob Rules* and *Dehumanizer* line-up of Black Sabbath reunite following the release of the compilation *Black Sabbath: The Dio Years* in 2007. By deciding not to call the band Black Sabbath—despite obvious financial incentives to do so—the band was able to record an album, 2009's *The Devil You Know*, which stood on its own terms. They also avoided the expectations of a Black Sabbath tour in which they would "have to" play the Ozzy-era classics like

"Paranoid."[11] While some fans persisted in calling the band Black Sabbath for obvious reasons, they had no right to expect the band to fit that name. The band could not be accused of any deceit on this front, because they went out of their way to shed the Black Sabbath name (while instead choosing a name that merely invoked the first album with Dio).

Sick and Tired ... of Changes

Fans may not like it when the line-up of their favorite band changes, even if the quality and style of the music remain high. While the music may be the most important thing for many fans, we also develop an attachment to the musicians who make it. Even though Tim "Ripper" Owens sounded very close to Rob Halford when he sang the Judas Priest classics, it just wasn't the same. Neil Murray is no less a bass player than Geezer Butler; Cozy Powell was just as amazing a drummer as Bill Ward; and Ronnie James Dio was a more gifted singer than Ozzy Osbourne. Still, some fans are not satisfied with "as good" or even better. They want to hear and see the musicians they grew up listening to in the bands they love, and we can certainly sympathize with their disappointment.

Nonetheless, as we've seen, a band has no obligation to the fans not to change its line-up, or to change its name if it does. Their only ethical obligation is to be upfront and honest about the change, and not to hide it behind deceptive marketing and advertising.[12] Ideally— in the absence of record company pressure and contractual obligations—artists can do what they want with their careers in terms of forming, changing, and breaking up bands, as well as playing the music they want to play. By the same token, though, fans have no obligation to remain loyal to a band as they're going through changes. There are Sabbath fans who only listen to the original line-up with Ozzy, or the Dio years, or the (underrated) Tony Martin era, and these are all valid choices. There is no reason that a fan has to appreciate all the line-ups and all the albums equally to be a "real" Sabbath fan, especially when each line-up is a distinct entity— and when we have the *Forbidden* album to test any "true" fan's devotion![13]

Notes

1. Well, 14 if you count Joe Satriani, who toured with the band in 1993 and 1994 but never recorded with them. And according to Joe Siegler's Black Sabbath website, www.black-sabbath.com, *30* musicians have served in Sabbath over the years, though some never toured or appeared on recordings.
2. Death metal bands take this to the extreme, crafting logos so intricate and literally dripping with imagery that you can't tell what the band's name is!
3. Immanuel Kant, *Grounding for the Metaphysics of Morals*, trans. James W. Ellington (Indianapolis: Hackett, 1993), 421. (This is standard Academy pagination, available in any reputable edition of Kant's work.)
4. A variant of this formula, the Formula of the Law of Nature, is based on consistency of the maxim with other important ends, like the survival of humanity itself (ibid.). But it's hard to see how "Tony Iommi and friends" recording as Black Sabbath endangers that—no matter how much you don't like the *Forbidden* album!
5. Kant, *Grounding*, 429.
6. In a political context, this is known as Kant's *publicity* criterion; as he wrote in his 1795 essay "To Perpetual Peace: A Philosophical Sketch," "All actions that affect the rights of other men are wrong if their maxim is not consistent with publicity," in *Perpetual Peace and Other Essays*, trans. Ted Humphrey (Indianapolis: Hackett, 1983), 381.
7. At the time of this writing that is how things are shaping up, but, like other fans, I hold out hope that the rest of the group will come to terms with Bill Ward.
8. Tony Iommi with T.J. Lammers, *Iron Man: My Journey Through Heaven and Hell with Black Sabbath* (Cambridge, MA: Da Capo Press, 2011), 246. (Tony would, of course, realize this goal of a solo album with multiple singers in 2000 with *Iommi*.)
9. Ibid., 249.
10. Think of the damage that a radical change of style does to a band's reputation; for instance, see my chapter "Metallica Drops a *Load*: What Does a Band Owe Its Fans (and Vice Versa)?" in William Irwin, ed., *Metallica and Philosophy: A Crash Course in Brain Surgery* (Malden, MA: Blackwell, 2007), 199–209.
11. Even among the band members themselves, there is no universally agreed upon explanation for why they chose not to use the Black Sabbath name. One likely reason, though, was to avoid confusion with

the original line-up, which had recently been inducted into the Rock and Roll Hall of Fame. See Martin Popoff, *Black Sabbath FAQ: All That's Left to Know on the First Name in Metal* (Milwaukee: Backbeat Books, 2011), 295–314.

12. Case in point: Tony's very short-term employer Ian Anderson recently released a follow-up to the Jethro Tull classic *Thick as a Brick*; the album, *Thick as a Brick 2*, and the ensuing tour, were billed as "Jethro Tull's Ian Anderson," even though no other members of Tull are involved (and the band itself is still together).

13. This chapter is dedicated to my father, who introduced me to Sabbath as a wee lad, and with whom I've shared a passion for the band ever since. (Sadly, I have not yet convinced him of the brilliance of Cannibal Corpse, but I persevere.)

Part V

SYMPTOMS OF THE UNIVERSE

Chapter 14

Wicked World
The Politics of the Supernatural in Black Sabbath

Erich Christiansen

Images of the supernatural run throuhout Black Sabbath's lyrics, matching the dark, ominous chords, brutal riffing, and somberly reflective instrumental codas. In Sabbath's songs, we encounter Satan, demons, sorcery, and, on a few occasions, God himself. But why? Was the band simply trying to find subject matter as dark as the riffs they were creating? Were they trying to cash in on the kind of eerie feelings that make horror movies possible? Probably, to some extent. But what I'm going to argue is that this imagery was a reaction (whether conscious or subconscious) to their political and economic position as working-class people. For this reason we'll focus on the first album (when the band was still broke) and one song from the second album.

The members of the band come from the industrial Aston area of Birmingham, England. Just to paint a quick picture: around the time the group formed, Ozzy Osbourne worked in a slaughterhouse, while Tony Iommi worked as a cutter at a sheet metal factory where he lost the tips of two fingers. Given their bleak circumstances, it's not surprising that Sabbath's lyrics portray a world dominated by magical forces beyond our control.

Black Sabbath and Philosophy: Mastering Reality, First Edition. Edited by William Irwin.
© 2013 John Wiley & Sons, Inc. Published 2013 by John Wiley & Sons, Inc.

"People Got to Work Just to Earn Their Bread"

Disadvantaged and downtrodden people are frequently religious and superstitious. Why wouldn't they be? Their lives are controlled by mysterious forces largely beyond their control. As Karl Marx (1818–1883) describes the capitalist system, "the landowner and the capitalist, who as such are merely privileged and idle *gods*, are everywhere raised above the worker and prescribe laws for him."[1] It is not a stretch to recast these "gods" as "devils." In fact, Marx makes this connection himself:

> Just as in religion the spontaneous activity of human fantasy, of the human brain and heart, reacts independently as an alien activity of *gods or devils* upon the individual, so the activity of the worker is not his own spontaneous activity.[2]

Marx's system of thought described how capitalism works: it generates wealth for those in power by exploiting those who aren't. This happens because there is a class of people who own the means of production: the factories, the tools, the raw materials—anything that's needed to produce the goods a society needs. The people who aren't in this class own very little except their ability to do work. So they have to sell that work to the owners, who control the economy. The game is therefore played with a stacked deck; the owners control the economy, and the workers, owning no capital of their own, have to accept it if they want a job. As workers, what happens to us in our workday and how we get the pay we need to survive is largely out of our hands.

Religion might seem to be separate from economics, but Marx didn't think so. He argues that everything that happens in society ultimately originates in people's material needs. The economic system that provides for those needs largely determines what the rest of the society looks like: its political system, its art, its culture, its philosophical ideas, and its religion.[3] Marx says that this occurs largely "independent of th[e] will" of working people.[4] As he says, "The mode of production of material life conditions the general process of social, political, and intellectual life. It is not the consciousness of men that determines their existence, but their social existence that determines their consciousness."[5] So according to this account, you might think you have a certain political stand or religious belief because of a conscious decision you made—and maybe you do. But it's just as likely that your political stand or religious belief has arisen because it's what the system needs people to believe to stay in power—or, conversely, what the people out of power need to believe in order to survive under that system and keep it in place.

So I'm not claiming that when Geezer Butler wrote or Ozzy Osbourne sang about God and the devil it was consciously a form of social protest, let alone a Marxist one—although they did have some songs of social protest. But what I am claiming is that the way these songs see the world is consistent with the social and economic situation that shaped the members of Black Sabbath. The songs portray the world as run by forces beyond our control.

"Day of Judgment, God Is Calling"

So, what role does religion play in a society based on an unfair system of wealth and power? Usually, Marxists take the view that religion is a smokescreen that makes us concentrate on another world, a made-up world beyond ours, so that we'll accept the inequality and oppression that exists on earth. But Marx also has a slightly different angle, which he discusses in a famous passage that is often presented out of context. What usually gets quoted is the sentiment "Religion is the opium of the people," implying that religious belief is something dangerously addictive, something that makes you numb and unaware. But the full context of the passage shows a more nuanced, more sympathetic view of the role of religion in the lives of working people.

> *Religious* suffering ... is an *expression* of real suffering and a protest against real suffering. Religion is the sigh of the oppressed creature, the sentiment of a heartless world, and the soul of soulless conditions. It is the *opium* of the people.[6]

Max Horkheimer (1895–1973) takes this analysis even further:

> The concept of God was for a long time the place where the idea was kept alive that there are other norms besides those to which nature and society give expression in their operation. Dissatisfaction with earthly destiny is the strongest motive for acceptance of a transcendental being.

> If justice resides with God, then it is not to be found in the same measure in the world. Religion is the record of the wishes, desires, and accusations of countless generations.[7]

Taken together, these passages suggest that religion isn't simply a con game in which the rulers pull the wool over the eyes of working people (even though it is also that). The problems of this world are the motivation to believe in another, better world. Religion is embraced by disadvantaged and downtrodden people because it gives them a world that is an alternative to the one they live in. If they seem to lack the power to achieve justice in their own lives, people can at least imagine that there is a powerful being that can bring them justice in the next life—or maybe, if they're lucky, even answer a prayer for help on earth. Religion shows there are values and standards that people can live by other than the rules that they have to follow at work, or that are passed by politicians. If religion is the opium of the people, we should remember that opium relieves our pain and makes us dream.

All right—but what does this have to do with Black Sabbath? Their first few albums only mention God a handful of times, but Satan is often present. Shouldn't we be focusing on that?

Indeed we should. But we have to extrapolate because while philosophers have discussed God for millennia they have rarely discussed Satan. The Devil is apparently seen as too much of a superstition, an irrational part of the religious tradition that philosophers no more need to argue against, let alone analyze, than goblins or elves. But in the Christian tradition, understanding the Devil is very important. If belief in God paints a picture of what we hope for and dream of, then Satan symbolizes the world we have, with all the suffering and evil that we experience in it.

Many Christians believe our world is dominated by Satan, ruled by the forces of evil. The song "Lord of this World" (from the album *Master of Reality*) takes its title image directly from these kinds of descriptions. Songs about devils are the horrific images of the nightmare we live in. Not only that, but the more evil the rulers of the world seem, the farther away God and his envisioned kingdom of justice seem. We'll see this is the case in Sabbath's lyrics: God is an entity finally cried out to in desperation, but not intimately experienced, or even necessarily loved. This is where the occult comes in; the desperate person appeals to any powerful being he can, including demons.

Bearing all this in mind, let's look at Sabbath's imagery on their first album.

"Black Sabbath"

Of course, no one does sonic darkness like Black Sabbath. That's why we love them. But my purpose isn't to analyze the music; rather, it's to examine the lyrical themes that give the emotions behind the music their content. The song "Black Sabbath" famously opens: "What is this that stands before me? / Figure in black which points at me / Turn round quick and start to run / Find out I'm the chosen one."

This image is based on a real experience. Geezer Butler, though a Catholic, had an interest in Satanism, and borrowed a book on witchcraft from Ozzy. As legend has it, Geezer put the book on the shelf and went to bed. When he woke, he saw a black figure standing at the foot of his bed. A moment later, the figure was gone—and so was the book.

We can interpret this image of the obscure, threatening figure, as a personification of the dark, obscure forces that hover over and threaten working peoples' existence. There's the figure of the looming foreman, and the potentially arbitrary power he can wield. There's the image of the higher bosses, powers that one may never see, handing down edicts of fate. There is the toxic smoke, billowing from factory smokestacks like something fuming from the gates of hell. There are the smells in the air of cow carcasses, of sulfur, or of other unnamed chemicals, bearing unknown poisons like the powers of the air.

We should also note the possibility for the overlap of Christianity and black magic. The move from one to the other is more common than one might think. The connection is based on the point of my main argument: working people often feel powerless over their lives, so they reach out to any forces that might be able to help them. It might start out with a prayer to God, or a rosary to the Virgin Mary. But if these official sources can't, or won't, help us with our plight, there are other, darker forces that very well may.

Anthropologist Edward Moody observed that although contemporary Satanists didn't have a particular class orientation, they did seem to have another common denominator.

The only characteristic common to all the members he observed was a behavioral trait that placed them outside of the cultural "norm." Many of them displayed a lack of knowledge of the "rules of the social game" and often felt unable to "make the system respond."[8]

We can see how this analysis might apply to class politics: the occult appeals to people who can't "make the system respond," those who can't make institutions work for them, because the institutions were never designed for them in the first place.

As the musical tension in "Black Sabbath" builds, the populace is terrified and we see "people running 'cause they're scared." As Satan "Watches those flames get higher and higher," the singer despairingly exclaims, "Oh no, no, please God help me!" But while Satan and demons play prominent roles in three songs on the first album, this is the only mention of God.

"The Wizard"

The appeal of magic is further explored in the second song on the debut album, "The Wizard." Geezer Butler told *Metal Sludge*, "I was reading *Lord of the Rings* at the time and I just based the lyrics on that. Gandalf."[9] But there is also a persistent story, circulated among fans, that the character is based on the band's drug dealer.[10] Whatever the accuracy of this latter interpretation, I think the fact that this story is widely believed says something interesting about the demographic that Black Sabbath speaks to. And, in fact, these two readings can be merged because they share something in common. The debate over recreational drugs is similar to the debate over fantasy literature (although the legal stakes are obviously very different). The opponents of drugs and fantasy literature see these things as escapism, potentially harmful or shallow denials of reality. Their proponents say that each of these can provide enlightenment and understanding by presenting a new perspective from which to view the world we live in, one transformed by imagination. Whichever side turns out to be right, it still fits with our thesis. If working people need to escape into drug-induced or fantasy worlds, it's because their reality is one that can't be consciously endured. And if these things, on the other hand, provide unique insights, it's because working people have not been able to get those kinds of insights from the institutions that form the superstructure arching over their oppression.

In "The Wizard" Ozzy sings, "Evil powers disappear / Demons worry when the wizard is near / He turns tears into joy / Everyone's happy when the wizard walks by." The song depicts a benign aspect of the supernatural: magic powers bring happiness and joy rather than terror. In fact, the wizard stands in opposition to demons. But notice the contrast: here a mortal sorcerer stands opposed to demons, whereas in Christianity one would appeal to God in such a battle. Presumably, the remote, authoritarian God of officially sanctioned religion seems too distant to help in earthly struggles. The gambit here seems to be to try the more hands-on approach of magic, rather than the uncertain assurances of prayer. If we compare this to "Black Sabbath," we can surmise that God is only called out to in the deepest desperation, when all other avenues have failed.[11] And we may begin to suspect that a God too remote and abstract to be truly loved or venerated, is actually an image concocted and fantasized by desperate people.

"N.I.B."

The song starts with a seduction: "Some people say my love cannot be true / Please believe me, my love, and I'll show you / I will give you those things you thought unreal / The sun, the moon, the stars all bear my seal." The person addressed may be a woman, but we can interpret the song more broadly. There are more kinds of seduction, and more kinds of love, than just romantic ones. In the song, more promises are made, and there appears to be acceptance, because the speaker says, "Now I have you with me, under my power / Our love grows stronger now with every hour / Look into my eyes, you'll see who I am / My name is Lucifer, please take my hand."

The seducer is revealed to be, again, Satan himself—called by his pre-fall angelic name of Lucifer. The seduction diabolically mirrors the Christian message; both promise eternal love, both promise a world the recipient of the message considered "unreal." In the Christian message, it's unseen heaven, and in this sales pitch, it's the actual universe itself—which it would be unreal for anyone to own. As it turns out, Satan offers his followers power over this world, but they receive only his power over them.

The reason that Satan is in any position to plausibly offer someone the universe is that the material world is seen as fallen, and therefore under Satan's control. This is why the sun, moon, and stars all bear his seal—they are now under his administration. So let's look at the nature of temptation in this context.

People who are struggling for their own existence and to make a good life for their families are constantly beset by temptations. They try to maintain their dignity and integrity, but the forces of economic imperatives often seem overwhelming to them. The questions are nagging: should I take a job as a scab, and feed my family, but betray the rest of my community? Should I take a job at a place that does something I don't believe in? Should I stab my friend in the back if it will get me a promotion? Should I dabble in crime to supplement my income? Should I join the army for the enlistment bonus, even though they might command me to kill someone I have no quarrel with—that is, if I don't die myself? But as "N.I.B." suggests, Lucifer is holding all the cards anyway. Even if I take the baubles he dangles in front of me, I just get deeper under his power.

This theme of a world under Satan's control leads us into the "Wicked World."

"Wicked World"

Over a grinding riff—as in the daily grind—Ozzy intones: "The world today is such a wicked place / Fighting going on between the human race / People got to work just to earn their bread / While people just across the sea / Are counting their dead." Here, the fundamental condition of the earth is that of sin and evil, immersed in factional violence. The depiction of workers laboring for a subsistence wage ("just to earn their bread") is paired with the image of people in other countries being killed en masse in war. Presumably, these topics are paired because the wars are being fought to increase the wealth and power of those who run the society. Therefore, the working people of foreign lands are targeted, and the working people of the imperialist countries are the ones who will be forced to go and fight. Martin Popoff describes the song's subject matter succinctly as going between "the fate of folks just working and then dying when politicians figure it's time for battle."[12]

"Wicked World" continues to highlight the divide between those who have power and those who don't. "A politician's job they say is very high / 'Cos he has to choose who's got to go and die / They can put a man on the moon quite easy / While people here on earth are dying of old diseases." This bitterly ironic portrait shows little sympathy for the supposedly difficult job of the politician who decides the fate of the working people he is sending to die for his own gain. His lack of concern is shown by the fact that he would rather fund scientific research to push forward space exploration than eradicate diseases that have plagued humanity for millennia.

Meanwhile, the next verse depicts the plight of the poor: "A woman goes to work every day after day / She just goes to work just to earn her pay / Child sitting crying by a life that's harder / He doesn't even know who is his father." The daily struggle for existence is carried on by a single mother trying to provide for her child, while the social safety net that could come to their aid is being squandered on war and space adventures. The last line could be addressing the economic problem associated with children being born out of wedlock in poor communities. But perhaps instead the real reason the child will never know his father is that his father was one of the people killed in the war, leaving this family behind.

Thus with "Wicked World," the landscape of the first album becomes more cohesive. The satanic threat is not just the spiritual one that haunts the Christian religion. In "Wicked World," we see that the satanic powers that rule the world are those of the moneyed interests that control all the world's institutions, demonically doling out death and suffering to working people.

The wars that these dark powers are responsible for lead us into the next album, 1971's *Paranoid*, and its first song, the masterpiece "War Pigs."

"War Pigs"

Even though the members of Black Sabbath are British, the war being waged by America in Vietnam was very much of concern to them. "War Pigs" starts with a clear image of the satanic nature of those who run the military and the government it serves: "Generals gathered in their masses / Just like witches at black masses / Evil minds that plot destruction / Sorcerers of death's construction."

Those in power are portrayed as sorcerers, summoning dark forces that they can barely control to carry out their terrible plans. From the ghostly, we go to the concrete site of destruction: "In the fields the bodies burning / As the war machine keeps turning / Death and hatred to mankind / Poisoning their brainwashed minds."

Like practitioners of the black arts, those in power conjure up destructive forces; the orders they give are like spells cast. Like evil wizards, they seem to practice mind control, turning conscious beings into servants who do their bidding and whose lives will be risked: "Politicians hide themselves away / They only started the war / Why should they go out to fight? / They leave that all to the poor."

No illusions here: the wars are being fought in the interests of the rich, to expand their economic power and crush opposition to this expansion. This image is reinforced by the name given to the rulers. They are called War *Pigs*, connoting obesity, over-consumption, and filthy lowness. One can picture the cigar-puffing, double-chinned profiteers, fat on other people's blood. But this state of affairs is prophesied not to last forever: "Treating people just like pawns in chess / Wait 'til their judgment day comes, yeah!"

After the tension mounts into an instrumental break, the slamming riff returns with the next verse, which features an apocalyptic fantasy of the final judgment: "Now in darkness, world stops turning / Ashes where their bodies burning / No more war pigs have the power / Hand of God has struck the hour / Day of Judgment, God is calling / On their knees, the war pigs crawling / Begging mercy for their sins / Satan, laughing, spreads his wings."

The singer revels in picturing the suffering that one day will be inflicted on those who have caused so much suffering themselves. But let's not forget that this is opium for the people, a pain reliever, a fantasy born out of the perceived inability to do anything about it in the real world. The warlords at whose whim ordinary people live and die are portrayed as demonic, because that is, indeed, how the obscure machinations of their apparently unlimited power must seem. The only alternative, then, is to call for help to God, a being with even greater, and possibly even more incomprehensible, power.

We've already seen Marx describing religion as an idea that makes an unbearable existence bearable. This is one of the main ways: as an articulation of the dream of justice finally being done in an unjust world. But the point here, in terms of my main thesis, is that this fantasy of being avenged by an unearthly power comes from the perceived inability of working people to stop it on our own. Ozzy's final exclamation of "Oh! Lord, yeah!" sounds triumphant in the context of Armageddon. But considering the condition that gives rise to it, we can interpret the whole scene as a call for help. According to Paul Wilkinson, "you really get the impression he's saying 'Lord, is there anything you can do about this?'"[13] However, even then, even if the longed-for help were to come, it would still end up being a cosmic battle, waged by powers beyond human control. That is why, again, the story is told in supernatural imagery, whether divine or demonic.

It's also worth mentioning that neither in this song, nor anywhere else on the second album do we get a loving or adoring relationship to God.[14] God is just another one of those vast forces that are out of our reach—apparently, only to be called upon in desperation, as a last resort.[15]

Final Judgment

Depicting a world run by demonic forces beyond our reach, Black Sabbath expressed the pain, frustration, and disempowerment of the working class that Karl Marx explained. But when you view the world this way, you run a risk. Portraying your enemies as all-powerful, you run the risk of giving up the idea of changing things. If the world seems dire enough, then the desire for justice may be replaced by a desire for escape. This escape could take the form of drugs or religion, not as means to insight and revelation, but as ways of shutting out the immediate world.

That being said, Black Sabbath provides us with a visceral portrait of how it can feel to live in our society. They show us what it's like to *need* to escape. They capture our world's potential for darkness. What we do about that darkness is up to us.

Notes

1. Karl Marx, *Early Writings* (New York: McGraw-Hill, 1963), 75, emphasis added.
2. Ibid.,125, emphasis added.
3. Karl Marx, *A Contribution to the Critique of Political Economy*. www.marxists.org/archive/marx/works/1859/critique-pol-economy/preface.htm.

4. Ibid.

5. Ibid.

6. *Early Writings*, 43.

7. Max Horkheimer, *Critical Theory: Selected Essays* (New York: Continuum, 1975), 129.

8. Margot Adler, *Drawing Down the Moon* (Boston: Beacon Press, 1979), 331.

9. Sir Wendell Neeley, "20 Questions with Geezer Butler," *Metal Sludge* 26 April 2005, www.metalsludge.tv/home/index.php?option=com_content &task=view&id=256&Itemid=52.

10. Paul Wilkinson, *Rat Salad: Black Sabbath the Classic Years 1969–1975* (New York: Thomas Dunne Books, 2006), 46.

11. Of course, it might be argued that, depending on how closely we take the song to be modeled on Gandalf, the wizard could be an emissary of God, as Gandalf was. But I think that the unholy role usually ascribed to wizards in the Christian tradition, coupled with the bruising darkness of the riffing, speaks against such a reading.

12. Martin Popoff, *Black Sabbath FAQ: All That's Left to Know on the First Name in Metal* (Milwaukee: Backbeat Books, 2011), 88–89.

13. Wilkinson, 74.

14. It has been suggested to me that a possible exception to this is in the last verse of "Electric Funeral" from *Paranoid*, which says "Supernatural King takes earth under his wing." But this is not a reading I agree with. Given that the context is of souls about to be sent to hell after a nuclear holocaust, and given that believers in God tend to be more likely to ascribe the term "supernatural" to the ungodly, I think it's more likely that the wing in question belongs to the "King of this World," Satan.

15. This changes in "After Forever" on the next album, *Master of Reality*.

Chapter 15

"Demons, Dreamers, and Madmen"
Is Ozzy Going Insane?

Kevin McCain

Let's face it, Ozzy has never had a firm grip on sanity. To his credit, though, he seems to realize it, and in the song "Am I Going Insane?" he asks the title question repeatedly.[1] Assuming that Ozzy isn't merely "Snowblind" at the moment or simply suffering the effects of a little too much "sweet leaf," his condition is quite distressing. In fact, he wonders if he's a "schizophrene." Schizophrenics commonly hear voices and suffer from delusions of persecution. The trouble is that they can't always distinguish between delusion and reality. And, as with many mental illnesses, schizophrenia is often accompanied by denial. As they say, "it's not paranoia if they really are out to get you," and likewise "it's not schizophrenia if it's real." But in "Am I Going Insane?" Ozzy is wondering whether there may in fact be something wrong with him. He is wondering if he can trust his senses and his ability to reason.

Ozzy's Insanity and Descartes' Demon

The question of whether Ozzy can ever know whether he is insane or not falls under the purview of epistemology—the branch of philosophy that is concerned with the nature of knowledge. In fact Ozzy's predicament is similar to the skeptical scenarios described by the father of modern epistemology, René Descartes (1596–1650).

Black Sabbath and Philosophy: Mastering Reality, First Edition. Edited by William Irwin.
© 2013 John Wiley & Sons, Inc. Published 2013 by John Wiley & Sons, Inc.

Descartes recognized the problem that insanity poses for knowledge, speaking of "madmen, whose brains are so damaged by the persistent vapours of melancholia that they firmly maintain that they are kings when they are paupers, or say that they are dressed in purple when they are naked, or that their heads are made of earthenware or that they are pumpkins, or made of glass."[2] The problem is that such madmen often do not realize that they are out of touch with reality. And even if they were to question their perceptions they would not necessarily feel confident in the answers they received.

Descartes felt sure of his own sanity, but he felt less sure that he could tell the difference between dreams and waking life. It is a common experience to wonder in the midst of a dream whether it is indeed a dream and to mistakenly conclude that it is not a dream. So really, all of life could just be a dream. Or worse, it could be the work of a malicious demon. Now, that sounds like Black Sabbath. The demon could constantly deceive us, much as a virtual reality program like The Matrix might trap and deceive us. If such a demon sought to deceive Descartes about everything, it doesn't seem that there would be any way for Descartes to know that the demon was causing all of his experiences. How could he tell what's real?

Descartes' situation with respect to his demon is similar to Ozzy's situation when he is trying to determine whether he is insane. If Ozzy has to ask "Am I going insane?" this means that he can't tell whether his experiences are the result of his insanity or whether they come about in the normal way. So, Ozzy ends up with a sort of universal doubt. And, Ozzy's situation may be worse than Descartes'. Descartes recognizes that it's possible that he is being deceived by a demon, but he doesn't really have any reason to think that he *actually* is so deceived. Ozzy, on the other hand, might have reasons for thinking that he is insane. After all, according to Ozzy, everybody's looking at him, he feels like going under, and he thinks he's a schizo. Despite their differences, perhaps a solution to Descartes' skeptical worry could offer a way for Ozzy to determine whether he is going insane.

How Not to Fall "Into the Void" of Skepticism

Skepticism, whether it is of the sort that Descartes presents or something akin to Ozzy's predicament, threatens our knowledge of the world around us. For example, you probably think you know that you are reading a book right now. How do you know this? What reason do you have for thinking that you are reading a book? Most likely, you have reasons such as your memories of what books look and feel like and your current visual and tactile experiences. However, the possibility of skeptical scenarios like Descartes' demon or the sort of insanity that may be afflicting Ozzy threaten the quality of your reasons. According to skeptics, you don't have better reasons for thinking that you are reading a book than you do for thinking that a demon is tricking you into thinking you are reading a book or for thinking that you are insane and confused about what is going on. Since you don't have better reasons for thinking you are reading a book than you do for thinking some such skeptical scenario obtains, the skeptic claims that you can't know you are reading a book. If the skeptic is right, the same sort of challenge is applicable to all of your beliefs about the world. So, if the skeptic is correct, Ozzy isn't the only one who has a problem—*you* don't know anything about the world around you!

Fortunately for you (and maybe for Ozzy—we'll see how things work out for him in a bit) a promising response to skepticism exists. Our commonsense view of the world offers a very good explanation of our sensory experiences. According to our commonsense view, the reason that you are having the sort of sensory experiences you are at this moment with their involuntary, spontaneous character, their coherence with one another, and their fit with your voluntary behaviors is that those sensory experiences are caused by an external world that contains mostly stable objects that can affect your sensory organs in a regular fashion. To illustrate, the commonsense explanation of your current experience of reading a book is that there is a real object in your possession—a book, which is exerting pressure on your hand as you hold it and it is affecting your eyes when you look at it. It is for this reason that your experience of the book now and your experience of it a few minutes from now or hours from now when you pick it up again will be very similar to one another.

Although our commonsense view of the world explains the features of our sensory experiences very well, the mere fact that it does so is not enough to keep us from falling "Into the Void" of skepticism. It must also be the case that our commonsense view of the world is the best available explanation of the features of our sensory experiences, and thus, a better explanation than the various skeptical scenarios. After all, if some skeptical scenario provides just as good of an explanation of our experiences as our commonsense view, why should we think one explanation is more likely to be correct than the other? Fortunately, our commonsense view is a better explanation than the various skeptical scenarios (at least for us—Ozzy's situation may be a bit worse depending on the sorts of answers he receives when he asks "am I going insane?").

While the case for thinking that our commonsense view of the world is the best explanation can be quite complicated, the gist of the matter is straightforward.[3] To see this, compare the commonsense explanation of your experience of reading this book presented above to the demonic explanation Descartes considered. According to the demonic explanation, your book experiences are caused by a demon deceiving you into thinking that you are currently reading a book. For one thing, our commonsense explanation is much richer than the demonic explanation. What would happen if you drop this book on your toe? (Not that I recommend you do so, but you could try it out just to check if you want.) The commonsense explanation tells us you are going to feel pressure on your toe when it looks to you that the book makes contact with it, and it might hurt if you aren't wearing shoes. What does the demonic explanation tell us? Nothing. It simply tells us after the fact that the experience you had when you dropped the book was caused by the demon. This is an important difference. Our commonsense view allows us to accurately predict the sorts of experiences that we will have. The demonic explanation doesn't allow us to make these sorts of predictions; it can only accommodate them after the fact. This makes our commonsense view a better explanation. This fact about predictions is true of other skeptical scenarios as well. The dreaming scenario doesn't allow us to make accurate predictions, nor do insanity scenarios. A further advantage the commonsense view has over skeptical scenarios is that the skeptical scenarios raise a number of unanswerable questions that the commonsense view doesn't. Think about the demonic explanation. It raises a number of questions that it cannot answer: Why is the demon deceiving you? How does it deceive you? Where did it come from? Where are you while the demon is deceiving you? How many demons are deceiving you—is it just the one or do they work in shifts? And so on. Other skeptical scenarios raise similar questions: How long have I been dreaming this dream? Have I ever been awake? What's keeping me alive while I dream? When did I start going insane? What is causing my insanity? If I'm insane, what is making my experiences continue to be coherent with one another? These unanswerable questions count against the skeptical scenarios.

Our commonsense view of the world is a better explanation. Thus, we have a way out of the skeptical predicament. Perhaps skepticism isn't much of a problem and we can know plenty of things about the world around us just as we thought. Everything seems good. Now that we've seen there is a good response to the threat of skepticism, as Black Sabbath tells us in "The Wizard," the "Sun is shining / Clouds have gone by" and now we can all "give a happy sigh." Right? Well, things seem pretty good for us when it comes to responding to skepticism, but what about Ozzy? Can he avoid falling prey to skepticism too? Things may not be so bright and shiny for Ozzy when he's "going through changes" and has to ask us "am I going insane?"

What Can Ozzy Know?

As we've seen, there is a way for us to escape from the threat of skepticism because our commonsense view of the world is the best explanation for why we have sensory experiences of the sort that we do. But, will this work for Ozzy? We don't have any reason to think that Descartes' demon actually exists, but maybe Ozzy does have reason to think that he is, or at least might be, going insane. After all, Ozzy asks many times "tell me people / Am I going insane?" What if there is no one to answer his question? What if Ozzy gets different answers to this question? Does it make a difference whether the people tell Ozzy "no" or "yes"? Can Ozzy ever know anything about the world around him now that he questions his own sanity? Tough questions.

There are four situations that Ozzy might encounter when he says "tell me people / Am I going insane?" He can receive no answer at all, perhaps because he is alone; everyone he asks can tell him "no"; everyone he asks can tell him "yes"; or some of those he asks can tell him "no" and some tell him "yes." If there is no one around to answer him, Ozzy is in a similar situation to us when we simply wonder whether we might be deceived by Descartes' demon or if we wonder if we are going insane. We can reasonably think that we aren't deceived by a demon and we aren't going insane because we have a better explanation—our commonsense view of the world. Although Ozzy might be a little less sure that he isn't going insane because he starts with doubts that we normally don't, he can still reasonably think that he isn't going insane. That would be the best explanation for why his experiences have the features that they do (assuming of course that his experiences have features similar to ours—if they don't, all bets are off!). So, if Ozzy is alone and his experiences are normal, he can reasonably answer his own question negatively.

The situation is similar when everyone assures him that he isn't going insane. Again, Ozzy can reason that the best explanation of the features of his experiences in general and for the fact that everyone testifies to him that he isn't going insane, is that he really isn't going insane. As long as the people telling him that he isn't going insane don't pop in and out of existence or look like ghosts or demons, Ozzy has good reason to think that he isn't going insane.

Things are not so promising when Ozzy is in one of the other possible situations. When Ozzy is in a situation where he gets mixed answers to his question, what should he think? This is tough. On the one hand, Ozzy's sensory experiences give him some reason to think that he isn't going insane and so does the testimony he receives from the people who tell him that he isn't going insane. On the other hand, the testimony that Ozzy receives from people telling him he is going insane gives him some reason to think that he is going insane. What is the verdict? As the great oracle, the Magic 8 Ball, often says "outlook uncertain." At best, Ozzy will have reason to think that he isn't going insane, but he will have less reason to think this than when everyone tells him he isn't. So, perhaps he can know things about the world around him, but he should be less sure of them than we should. At worst, Ozzy will be in nearly the same situation as when everyone tells him that he is going insane. But, is that bad enough to mean he lacks knowledge of the world around him?

In the situation where everyone tells Ozzy that he is going insane, he has reason to think that he is indeed going insane. As a result of this, Ozzy will now have reason to doubt that his experiences are accurate and to doubt his own reasoning ability. This suggests that Ozzy won't be able to have knowledge of the world around him because all of the reasons he might have in support of beliefs about the world around him will be defeated. For instance, an experience of a figure in black pointing at him will be easily dismissed by the fact that he has good reason to think that his experiences are not good indicators of how things actually are. Consequently, Ozzy can't know anything about the world around him. Well, you might think that Ozzy can at least know that the answer to his question "am I going insane?" is "yes." But, he can't know that either! He can't trust his experiences and he can't even trust his own reasoning—reasoning that he must utilize in order to conclude that the answer to the question "am I going insane?" is "yes." Further, in this situation Ozzy can't even know that people have answered his question positively because in order to know this he has to rely on his experiences of them telling him he's going insane, and these are experiences that he can't trust. So, you might think that if Ozzy lands in this situation he really is "lost in the wheels of confusion." He can't know anything about the world around him! It's no wonder that he doesn't sound very cheerful.

Should we hold an "Electric Funeral" for Ozzy's knowledge of the world around him? Encourage him to hide "Behind the Wall of Sleep" and escape the "Wicked World"? Not yet. If Ozzy's experiences are like ours, then the best explanation of why he has them might still be that the world is largely how he takes it to be. If so, then Ozzy might still be in a position to know at least some things about the world around him, even if he has reason to think that he is going insane. Perhaps even in this darkest situation Ozzy can have some knowledge of the world around him.

Is This Cause to Be Paranoid?

Ozzy's situation is a bit disconcerting. But is it a reason to "find a place to hide"? Should it make him "feel like going under"? No. There's no need to be "Paranoid" or to think that "Solitude" is the answer. So, before you "go home—sit down and moan" remember that Ozzy only lands in the severe skeptical situation when a number of elements are in place: he has reason to think that he is going insane, he asks "am I going insane?" and he is told by several people "yes." Additionally, his experiences fail to provide him with reasons to think that he knows some things about the world around him. Without all of these in place Ozzy can retain at least some knowledge of the world around him, and thus avoid falling prey to extreme skepticism. Merely avoiding extreme skepticism isn't much of a victory though because his situation may still land him in a state where he can't know much at all. Of course, it could be that everything I've said here is mistaken and Ozzy is just fine. It could be that I haven't written anything at all. It could be that there is no book to be read. It could be that I'm sitting all alone imagining all of this …. "Tell me people, am *I* going insane?"

Notes

The title of this chapter comes from Harry G. Frankfurt, *Demons, Dreamers, and Madmen: The Defense of Reason in Descartes's Meditations* (Princeton: Princeton University Press, 2007).

1. Of course Ozzy may not be speaking for himself personally in this song. He may instead be presenting a persona, a narrator.
2. René Descartes, *Meditations on First Philosophy with Selections from the Objections and Replies*, trans. John Cottingham (Cambridge: Cambridge University Press, 1986), [I, 19].
3. For a more complete account of why our commonsense view is the best explanation see Jonathan Vogel, "Cartesian Skepticism and Inference to the Best Explanation," *Journal of Philosophy* 87 (1990), 658–666.

Chapter 16

"As the War Machine Keeps Turning"
Just War Theory, Pacifism, and the War on Terror

Jacob M. Held

When we think of anti-war protest songs the first image that comes to mind is probably John Lennon or some group of hippies or peaceniks singing "Give Peace a Chance," "All You Need Is Love," "For What It's Worth," or perhaps the more upbeat "Fortunate Son." What doesn't immediately come to mind is Black Sabbath. But "War Pigs" is an iconic anti-war song, and Geezer Butler, who wrote the lyrics, is a peacenik.[1] In fact, "War Pigs" is the first in a long line of heavy metal anti-war songs, from Iron Maiden's lamentations in "2 Minutes to Midnight," and "Run to the Hills," to Metallica's remorse over lost life and superfluous suffering in "Disposable Heroes" and "One." Heavy metal is rife with anti-war messages, often infused with anger at the pointless pain and suffering caused by wars waged for no good reason by "Generals gathered in their masses . . . evil minds that plot destruction . . . making war just for fun" ("War Pigs").

It may surprise some people to discover that a lot of metal, which is typically perceived as hyper-masculine and violent, is actually anti-war.[2] But, as we'll see, Black Sabbath and many of their colleagues in metal are not only anti-war, but they can also help us to understand just war theory. It's just that they "*fight* for peace" instead of passively pleading for it.

Black Sabbath and Philosophy: Mastering Reality, First Edition. Edited by William Irwin.
© 2013 John Wiley & Sons, Inc. Published 2013 by John Wiley & Sons, Inc.

War Is Hell

Let's begin with a simple fact: war is an undeniable evil that causes incalculable suffering. Lives of combatants and non-combatants are lost; injuries, both physical and mental, both short and long term are incurred. No soldier returns from war unharmed. All soldiers carry the war forever within them, many suffering significant emotional traumas leading to substance abuse and failed relationships and marriages. "First it was the bomb, Vietnam napalm / Disillusioning, you push the needle in / From life you escape" ("Hand of Doom"). The human toll of war is profound and profoundly disconcerting. There is also the economic impact of lost revenue, resources that might have otherwise been spent on education, public works, or other social services. There is loss of infrastructure, buildings and roads, and there are citizens being turned away from their homes and becoming refugees in their own land. As Geezer Butler says, "Why would anyone care for Iraq when the American health system needs money? Why spend all the money that could help fix the problem in Iraq? We have enough poverty in our own countries we need to worry about before going anywhere else."[3]

War truly is a "game tailor made for the insane." So how do we justify it? (Yes, that was a quote from an Ozzy solo song, "Thank God for the Bomb." There will be more, and I'm not apologizing.)

At its most basic, war is mass killing. It always results in fields of bodies burning. So, on the one hand we feel morally compelled to justify treating people like pawns in chess. But on the other hand, war seems to be a condition where morality has broken down, where civilization has given way to barbarism and chaos, and so all our moralistic pretenses seem to go out the window. One might recall the famous dictum of General William Tecumseh Sherman (1820–1891), "War is Hell." Or his statement in a letter to the mayor and council of Atlanta, "War is cruelty, and you cannot refine it . . . ." War is cruel, and those who wage it are by definition sorcerers of death's construction. They can't do otherwise than orchestrate death and hatred to mankind. That's just how war is waged; it can't be done painlessly. So one interpretation of these claims is that "war is hell, because as in hell, the horrors know no bounds."[4]

Some people seem to think that war can't be governed by morality or law, and so at root war merely is about promoting one's interests in the face of a threat. Thus we find generals, like Sherman on his march to the sea, gathered in their black masses utilizing a policy of scorched earth, littering the land with bodies burning. But "even in hell, it is possible to be more or less humane, to fight with or without restraint."[5] We can't avoid moral reasoning, especially when dealing with a moral tragedy such as war. So the question becomes, if we must apply moral reasoning to war, how should we morally assess it?

Why Should They Go Out to Fight?

Justifying war is usually a two-part process, one must justify the right to go to war, and then one must justify how to fight. One must provide "an account of just cause and an account of just means."[6] The term used to indicate the just cause part of the account is *jus ad bellum*, Latin for the right to go to war. The term *jus in bello*, Latin for rights in war, is used to indicate the just means part of the account.

Jus ad bellum is about a nation's right to go to war. It's the justification for using lethal force on a massive scale. The standard account goes something like this: War is a necessary evil, so the presumption is always against war. You need to have a really, really, really good reason to overcome this presumption and justify the mass killing and serious evil you are about to inflict on the world. Those who want war have to make the case for war. "Time will tell on their power minds" if they "mak[e] war just for fun / Treating people just like pawns in chess." If you plan to start a war and leave the fighting to the poor, you still have to make a compelling case for your plan.

There are many formulations of the criteria one must meet in order to successfully plead for the use of military force, but most boil down to the following three criteria: 1. There must be a just cause for the use of such force. (The just cause may be self-defense, the defense of others, the protection of rights, or the maintenance of order.) 2. The use of force must be a last resort after all non-belligerent means of resolution have been exhausted. 3. The means you intend to use must be proportionate to the evil being staved off through your war action.[7]

Seemingly contradictory sentiments in some metal songs illustrate the point. Iron Maiden sings the praises of warrior virtues and courage in "The Trooper" and "Aces High," but then condemn war in "2 Minutes to Midnight" and "Run to the Hills." Black Sabbath seems clearly anti-war in "Wicked World," "War Pigs," "Children of the Grave," and "Electric Funeral," yet Ozzy sings a different tune in "Thank God for the Bomb." The apparent contradiction is resolved if we consider the justice of the war actions in the pro-war anthems, the injustice of the war in the anti-war songs, and the proportionality of the responses to the threats being faced. Clearly, Iron Maiden thinks World War I was justified, but the terror bombings in World War II and the slaughter of American Indians for Western expansion were unjustified. Black Sabbath condemns the use of atomic weapons like those used on Hiroshima and Nagasaki as excessive, and it condemns the Vietnam conflict as an unjust war. But Ozzy believes nuclear deterrence is a reasonable response to Soviet aggression or expansion. It's all about having a just cause and a proportionate response; that is, using just means to fight for your just cause.

Necessary Evil or Overkill?

Our moral work isn't done once we, or the politicians in charge, have decided who's got to go and die and for what purpose. Once the war is justified we have to discuss how we plan to wage it. Do we rain down "obscene fire," let loose the "atomic tide" and commit "the ultimate sin" of unleashing the "killer of giants"? Do we resort to overkill and sing the dirge of the electric funeral, or do we act with restraint? Even if war is a moral disaster, even if it is hell, there must be restrictions on how we prosecute it. The moral rubrics guiding behavior during war are *jus in bello*, or one's rights in war.

Even war initiated for a just cause does not justify any and all means to wage it. After all, part of *jus ad bellum* was making sure the destruction required to wage the war was proportionate, and once we're in the war this requirement still holds. War is a balancing act of weighing evils against each other. And the rubrics traditionally held to restrict our actions in war are the principles of proportion and discrimination. Here we assess our proposed action and ask if it is necessary in order to achieve a legitimate military objective. Anything more is overkill, superfluous or unnecessary suffering, and so unjustified.

In addition, we secure protection for non-combatants by declaring them off limits. Non-combatants must be shown due care and their interests acknowledged and respected, although their foreseeable deaths are excusable if they are the unintended result of necessary and proportionate military actions. I mean, you simply can't wage modern war without using a lot of things that make really big explosions in areas often populated by non-combatants. And since you can't evacuate everybody from all potential war zones, either you'll have to find a way to morally justify their deaths or not fight. And since fighting seems necessary at times, that leaves only a moral justification for the regrettable loss of innocent life.[8]

But proportion and discrimination are not just about making sure the numbers work out; that we kill more combatants than non-combatants or fewer non-combatants than we otherwise could have. If it were a simple numbers game one could justify (and historically people have) horrific practices such as the fire/terror bombings of Dresden and Tokyo[9] in World War II by simply claiming that fewer lives were lost than would've been had the terror bombings not continued, or that this massive loss of life is less horrendous than other forms of butchery we might inflict were we not to use this option.[10] This claim is difficult to support, and so it's not surprising that the loss of civilian life is often lamented in metal songs. "Body bags and little rags of children torn in two" ("2 Minutes to Midnight") "raping the women . . . enslaving the young and destroying the old" ("Run to the Hills"), or "you children of today are children of the grave" ("Children of the Grave").

The principles of proportion and discrimination are significant moral checks on how we wage war. One scholar notes that if a war can't be fought while respecting the principles of proportion and discrimination, then it can't be justified in the first place, implying just cause is bound by just conduct. He asks, "Why should we think that a war that cannot, or is unlikely to, be waged with just tactics should ever be considered a just war from the outset?"[11] Because this idea has traction, pacifists maintain that no wars can be justified. In other words, the way war is waged is necessarily disproportionate to the threat and is always disrespectful of the principle of discrimination.

Until the Day the War Drums Beat No More

Pacifists generally argue that the cost of war is unjustifiable. The images drawn in "Wicked World," "War Pigs," and "Electric Funeral" get the point across quite well, especially if one considers the threat of nuclear war. Wars result in hundreds of thousands and even millions of deaths, mass exoduses, refugee crises, billions and billions of dollars of damage, and long-term social and economic problems. Beyond fields of bodies burning in "War Pigs," Sabbath depicts even worse horrors in "Electric Funeral" as "the atomic tide / . . . / Turns houses into sty / Turns people into clay / Radiation minds decay." From this perspective, the enormity of war is unjustifiable.

A simple proportionality calculus, comparing the goods of war against the evils of war, justifies pacifism. Rarely, if ever, in history has a war led to fewer deaths than surrender or pacifism would have. One scholar illustrates this through the example of World War II. Estimating that the allied share of deaths, both combatant and non-combatant was around six and one-half million, he states, "No one denies that a Nazi victory in World War II would have had morally frightful results. But, according to anti-war pacifism, killing six and one-half million people is also morally frightful, and preventing one moral wrong does not obviously outweigh committing another."[12] If we take proportionality to simply be about the total number of deaths or the total calculation of destruction, war is incredibly difficult to justify. Surrender would probably lead to less pain and less suffering.

But is it only about death and destruction, or is there a further value being fought for when one thinks about justifying war? Isn't sovereignty or self-determination valuable? Wouldn't rule under Nazis be problematic in itself? As Sabbath urges us, "love is still alive you must be brave." You "win the fight for peace or . . . disappear" ("Children of the Grave").

Perhaps self-defense isn't a good excuse in some cases. Perhaps losing a small, inconsequential island is not worth millions of lives. Maybe sometimes it is more cost effective and more humane to accept defeat than to fight.[13] But even acknowledging this possibility doesn't deny that there might be some cases that pass a threshold of intolerable evil. Nazis probably pass this threshold. If they don't, who could?

Reasonable people may disagree. Self-determination and rights may hold no value to some, whereas others see them as constitutive of the value of human life.[14] "Justice and Liberty, you can buy but you don't get free," as Bruce Dickinson sings in "Born in '58." And it's "Liberty or death, what we so proudly hail" as Metallica claims in "Don't Tread on Me." How you live is as important as that you live. So to dismiss sovereignty as a value is to dismiss something considerable to many reasonable and thoughtful people.

But we shouldn't be dismissive of the pacifist's response to traditional just war theorizing. After all, what some might term war crimes, and what are surely horrendous acts of brutality, such as the terror bombings of Germany in World War II and the atomic attacks on Hiroshima and Nagasaki, have been justified within this traditional theoretical framework. We should be wary of those who respond to modest and even grave threats with Ozzy's refrain from "Thank God for the Bomb": "Nuke 'ya, Nuke 'ya." Pacifism serves as a very important moral check on our war making. We can see this clearly if we turn our eyes briefly to the war on terror.

When War Is Obsolete

The war on terror poses a real problem for traditional just war theory. You begin with the simple problem that you are no longer fighting another nation or its army, but rather a bunch of non-state actors, terrorists. Then you ask, how do you fight individuals? You can't declare war on them, and you can't just invade every country in which they happen to live. Should you even use military tactics? The other option is to use law enforcement. So, is fighting terrorism more like conducting a war, or is it more like fighting crime? Well, the answer is that it's like both, but not entirely like either. Terrorism is criminal activity, murder, conspiracy, vandalism, and the like. But it is also a national security threat, so it is similar to an invasion or the threat of a rogue nation. There's a lot of gray, and just war theory is not good with gray areas. Metallica's "All Nightmare Long" can be interpreted as saying that we should hunt terrorists down without mercy, all nightmare long. And you won't find a more enthusiastic hawk than Megadeth's Dave Mustaine who in "Amerikhastan" declares, "Hey Jihad Joe / Guess what? / We're coming to get you." A response seemingly justified if you truly believe "We are just a war away from Amerikhastan."[15] But Geezer Butler is clear when he says of "War Pigs" that "You can relate that to any war going on at any time. Unfortunately, wars are always with us. . . . Just look what is happening with the Iraq thing, with all the ordinary people dying over that crap."[16] So, we have some questions to resolve.

Should we treat terrorists as combatants?[17] Well, doing so poses some real problems. Soldiers aren't criminals, and they can't be tried for their actions. They are considered immune from prosecution unless they commit war crimes. Fighting is not a crime in a time of war, even if you are on the other side. Instead of being criminally prosecuted, soldiers are held prisoner until the cessation of hostilities. Then they are released. We can see the problem with terrorists. When are hostilities over? When are they no longer a threat? We should probably just prosecute them for crimes. But criminals have rights. You can't just assassinate them by sending drones to track them down while they sleep, or send in a commando hit squad. Criminals have to be arrested. Standards of evidence apply, and there must be due process and a trial. We don't want to grant these criminal rights to terrorists. So we treat them like whatever is most expedient at the moment, which is great if you're only worried about killing people, but it's not so great if you are worried about the judicious or limited use of force. If terrorists have no criminal rights, what protects them from unjust prosecution? If terrorists are not soldiers and so not afforded the protections of international law, what protects them from maltreatment? Their status, as "unlawful enemy combatants" is a fabrication that allows us to use all the power at our disposal without any legal checks and balances. Neither domestic nor international laws apply to them. They have no recourse to appeal their incarceration or treatment; there is no oversight, and so no protection from the abusive misuse of power. We classify terrorists in such a way that they are deprived of protection from national or international law; we treat them however we please; and we claim it's legal since no laws apply to them.[18] And we have to, right? We have to win the war on terror. Here is where the pacifist critique comes in handy.

"Win the Fight for Peace"

Can we justify the war on terror as a war? Well, is there just cause? One might claim it's a matter of self-defense, but even if we are under attack, proportion is still relevant and we must ask whether the potential damage we're threatened with justifies the response we've made. How many thousands have died or been wounded on our side? How many innocents in Iraq and Afghanistan? Let's not even start to think about the expenditure of resources. And for what? Are we any closer to victory? Is victory even possible? Here's the problem: you can't win a war on terror. You will never remove the threat. The world will never be one hundred percent secure; it can't be. As Hugo Grotius (1583–1645) noted, "Human life exists under such conditions that complete security is never guaranteed to us."[19] So if there is no hope for victory, any response is disproportionate and you have no moral justification for war. On these grounds alone the war on terror is morally bankrupt. But even assuming you could justify the cause of war, can you justify the means? Well, how is the war prosecuted? Simply put, the only way to wage the war is to target non-combatants intentionally, that is, to aim at people who support terror organizations or who we suspect of supporting terrorists. We target international criminals and suspected criminals and assassinate them, or more accurately institute a policy of extra-legal execution. When we do capture them, we torture them. And don't let the euphemism of "enhanced interrogation" confuse you. What we do would be actionable under the Geneva Convention were it done to a soldier. Waterboarding is torture, but since we reclassify terrorists as neither soldier nor criminal we get away with it. We create a loophole in the law to allow us to do what is illegal otherwise, but immoral nonetheless. The only way to wage a war on terror is to break all our traditional moral guidelines. But when we reach for extreme measures and try to justify the unjustifiable, we need to ask some difficult questions, such as: "Is fighting worth it if we have to fight this way?" and "Can this war be won, or do we lose by fighting just as surely as we would by surrendering?"

Sabbath dealt with the threat of atomic war in several songs, including "Electric Funeral" and "Children of the Grave," and Ozzy dealt with nuclear war and deterrence in "Thank God for the Bomb" and "Killer of Giants." All of these songs speak to the horror of unleashing unimaginable destruction on the world in the name of a hypothetically "just" war. And many deterrence theorists question whether a nuclear war could ever be justified. Some maintain that not fighting is the only sane response, even if it meant letting oneself be nuked. "It is a feature of massive retaliation that while there is or may be some rational purpose in threatening it, there could be none in carrying it out . . . the resulting war could not be won . . . We could only drag our enemies after us into the abyss."[20] The main threat today isn't the mushroom cloud of a killer of giants, it is terrorism, and our methods of fighting aren't to threaten a nuclear response but to practice the barbarity we historically have disparaged and prosecuted as war crimes. Just as Sabbath and Ozzy posed a pacifist check on the hawks that screamed "Nuke 'em," so should we pose a challenge to those who would so readily restrict civil liberties in the name of security.

Pacifism demands that if we can't wage a war justly then we simply don't wage a war. We have other ways to fight terrorism, so we must avoid unjust means. Otherwise, on our day of judgment, when God is calling, we'll surely be begging mercy for our sins. We had better learn from the example of war pigs now before we're all left groveling in the mud.[21]

Notes

1. See Chapter 8 "Wicked World: Geezer the Peacenik: Geezer Butler on War," in Martin Popoff, *Black Sabbath FAQ: All That's Left to Know on the First Name in Metal* (Milwaukee: Backbeat Books, 2011), 87–91.
2. This is not to say that all metal is anti-war. Clearly it's not. Just listen to Manowar's *Battle Hymns* for starters.
3. Martin Popoff, *Black Sabbath: Doom Let Loose* (Toronto: ECW Press, 2006), 34.
4. David Luban, "War Crimes: The Law of Hell," in Larry May, ed., with the assistance of Emily Crookston, *War: Essays in Political Philosophy* (New York: Cambridge University Press, 2008), 268.
5. Michael Walzer, *Just and Unjust Wars: A Moral Argument with Historical Illustrations* (New York: Basic Books, 2007), 33.
6. James P. Sterba, "Reconciling Pacifists and Just War Theorists," in Lewis Vaughn, *ed., Doing Ethics: Moral Reasoning and Contemporary Issues*, 2nd ed. (New York: W. W. Norton and Company, 2010), 629.
7. For a good, succinct, standard account of *jus ad bellum* and *jus in bello* see William V. O'Brien, *The Conduct of Just and Limited War* (New York: Praeger, 1981), especially Chapters 2 and 3.
8. This idea is known in the literature as the principle or doctrine of double effect. There are obvious issues with it such as: if you foresee the deaths and still proceed, didn't you really intend them? And if the deaths are regrettable and they are the necessary result of waging modern war, perhaps modern warfare is simply morally inexcusable and so we should all be pacifists.
9. The firebombing of Dresden and Tokyo killed an estimated 100 000 people each. Walzer, *Just and Unjust Wars*, 261, 266 respectively.

10. See Walzer, *Just and Unjust Wars*, Chapter 16 for an interesting discussion on this point.

11. Larry May, "The Principle of Just Cause," in May, *War: Essays in Political Philosophy* (Cambridge: Cambridge University Press, 2008), 65.

12. Douglas P. Lackey, "Pacifism," in William H. Shaw, ed., *Social and Personal Ethics*, 7th ed. (Boston: Wadsworth, Cengage Learning, 2011), 322.

13. For a discussion of this idea see Larry May, "The Principle of Just Cause," in May, *War: Essays in Political Philosophy*.

14. For an expression of this idea see Thomas Hurka, "Proportionality and Necessity," in May, *War: Essays in Political Philosophy* (Cambridge: Cambridge University Press, 2008), 142.

15. Megadeth, "Amerikhastan," from the *United Abominations* album. And there is an odd ambiguity here. The lyrics sometimes seem to indicate that the war on terror is leading to a loss of liberty and the destruction of our traditional American values. At other times it seems to indicate that the threat is terrorism. I think the proper reading is probably that both are threats, so being one war away from Amerikhastan could mean if we lose the war on terror the Islamo-fascists win. But it could also mean that the way in which we wage the war erodes our freedoms and turns us into the monsters we are fighting, extremists with no respect for liberty.

16. Popoff, *Black Sabbath: Doom Let Loose*, 34.

17. Some theorists have maintained that the old dichotomy of combatant and non-combatant is no longer accurate or useful and so we should instead use a graded scale based on level of participation to determine the level of guilt and so the permissibility of targeting a particular person. See, for example, Michael L. Gross, *Moral Dilemmas of Modern War: Torture, Assassination, and Blackmail in an Age of Asymmetric Conflict* (Cambridge: Cambridge University Press, 2010), especially Chapter 2.

18. For a good discussion of this point see David Luban, "The War on Terror and the End of Human Rights," in Vaughn, *Doing Ethics*, 2nd ed. (New York: W. W. Norton and Company, 2010), 728–734.

19. Cited in Gregory M. Reichberg, "Jus ad Bellum," in May, *War: Essays in Political Philosophy*, 27.

20. Walzer, *Just and Unjust Wars*, 274–275.

21. Many thanks to William Irwin for his helpful suggestions on an earlier version of this chapter.

Chapter 17

Stop Stereotyping Sabbath
Sex, Subjugation, and Stupidity

Robert Arp

The image of the caveman conjures up two ideas. The first is that cavemen are stupid, simplistic, even juvenile subhumans who "ooh ooh" around like apes, kind of half-communicating with each other and being utterly mesmerized by mundane things like fire and lightning flashes. In fact, the GEICO commercials where a caveman gets insulted by the slogan, "So Easy, A Caveman Can Do It," purposely play on this idea of the bewildered brute. The second idea is that cavemen are manly or even mean and misogynistic males with clubs who sneak up behind women, club them on the head, then drag them away to dominate them and violate them sexually. Just think of the Mel Brooks movie *History of the World, Part 1*, which features a scene where a caveman clubs a woman in a stereotypically troglodyte fashion.

When I was in graduate school studying for the Ph.D. in philosophy in the late 1990s, I got into a brief discussion with one of my philosophy professors before a seminar one night. The topic of music came up, and I told my prof that I loved heavy metal. He chuckled condescendingly and claimed something like the following, which I will never forget: "Heavy metal is the most base and simplistic form of pseudo-music written for adolescent boys who don't have any musical depth or creativity, let alone sexual self control. It's a lot of noise, numskulls, and nastiness, really." So, not only was my prof

Black Sabbath and Philosophy: Mastering Reality, First Edition. Edited by William Irwin.
© 2013 John Wiley & Sons, Inc. Published 2013 by John Wiley & Sons, Inc.

basically likening me to the typical caveman, but he was also expressing a fairly common heavy metal stereotype. The following quotation from a 1984 Robert Duncan book—one that my old philosophy prof would definitely agree with—is found reprinted and referenced all over the Web, in articles, and in books:

> Heavy metal: pimply, prole, putrid, unchic, unsophisticated, anti-intellectual (but impossibly pretentious), dismal, abysmal, terrible, horrible, and stupid music, barely music at all . . . music made by slack-jawed, alpaca-haired, bulbous-inseamed imbeciles in jackboots and leather and chrome for slack-jawed, alpaca-haired, downy-mustachioed imbeciles in cheap, too large t-shirts with pictures of comic book Armageddon ironed on the front . . .

But you hardly ever find reprinted what Duncan says a few lines later, which is this: "Heavy metal, mon amour, where do I start?"[1]

Black Sabbath is one of the pioneers of heavy metal, if not the band that started the whole genre. And since 1970 when their first album came out, for millions of people—myself included—Sabbath has been a definite amour. I was born in 1970, and my most vivid and profound memories of listening to music as a kid are associated with songs from the first three Sabbath albums, with the song "War Pigs" topping the list. Once, my older brother tried to scare me by playing the ending of "Children of the Grave" and calling me into his darkened room. But I wasn't scared. I absolutely loved Sabbath's music and was utterly captivated by it. Yet, I wouldn't consider myself the caveman type. I try to be intellectually curious and critically analytical about things in general, and I also try to be socially and morally thoughtful toward women in particular. Even as a pimply, alpaca-haired, adolescent prole listening to a cassette tape of *Sabbath Bloody Sabbath* on my Sony Walkman, I was always kind of a softy, somewhat pensive and sensitive to people's feelings. And I know there are many male Sabbath fans, who, like me, don't fit the caveman description in the least bit.

Let's Not Be Hasty Here . . .

So, the caveman description of the typical Sabbath fan is a stereotype or prejudice that results from the fallacy of hasty (or false) generalization. In general, a fallacy occurs when we inappropriately or incorrectly draw a conclusion in an argument from reasons that do not support the conclusion. The fallacy of hasty generalization occurs when someone inappropriately thinks, "if one, or a few, or even most are like that (premise), then they must *all* be like that (conclusion)." It's a fallacy because the conclusion that "they must all be like that" or "they all must have that same feature, quality, or characteristic" does not follow from and cannot be fully supported by reasons having to do with one, a few, or even most instances being "like that" or having the certain feature, quality, or characteristic.[2]

Hasty generalization is all too common in our thinking. Sally had one bad experience with a particular Toyota, so she never buys another Toyota again because she fallaciously thinks that the same bad experience will definitely result. (It's possible, but is it *definite*?) John will never go to any Wendy's ever again because he got bad service at the one on the corner of 5th and Main Streets. Thinking again about the manly, misogynistic "caveman" mentality that is exhibited by lots of metalheads, can we truly saddle all metalheads with those traits? Of course not. Perhaps, contrary to popular opinion, there have been many more meek, mild-mannered, moral metalheads over the years, than unbridled, unhinged, uncultivated, unethical ones.

So we've debunked the myth that *all* metalheads are morons, mean motherf-ers, or misogynists. Still, there could be something to these negative perceptions of metal and metalheads. Often there's a kernel of truth in stereotypes. In other words, stereotypes wouldn't become stereotypes if there weren't *some* truth to them.

Practically Clubbing Women

What about all of the sexual abuse and predation of women by male metalheads and other rock musicians? Both Ozzy Osbourne and Tony Iommi have claimed that they regularly had sex with groupies. Ozzy has stated, "It's every British band's dream to play the States. When we got there finally, we fucked as many groupies as we could,"[3] while Iommi has reminisced, "We came to L.A. to record, and we stayed at a house in Bel Air. At the end of the day, it was all dope, booze, drugs, fucking chicks. Oh, dear, we had some fun in that house."[4] A scene from the 2001 movie *Rockstar* does a great job of showing how the various groupies are literally lined up in the hallway—like products on an assembly line—waiting their turn to have sex with the members of Steel Dragon. Note, too, that the very term, "rock and roll," originally referred to the rocking and rolling associated with sex.

You don't need to be Sigmund Freud to know that a large percentage of men dominate women sexually through macho pressure or cheat on their girlfriends and wives. Some even commit rape.[5] The fairly new science of evolutionary psychology gives some insight into this male sexual tendency, having to do with the fact that men produce semen their whole lives, and are genetically programmed (to a certain extent) to want to spread their seed as much as possible to ensure the continuation of their genes.[6] Of course, even if this is true, there are straightforward moral reasons—as well as reasons having to do with your own survival and happiness—not to be diddling everyone you can get your hands on. Despite all his conquests, the fictional character Don Juan was ultimately mistrusted, lonely, and miserable . . . and I bet it burned when he peed, too!

As with drug abuse, there have been a number of studies linking heavy metal musicians, as well as those who listen to heavy metal, to caveman-clubbing, predatory, abusive sexual behavior.[7] Even more studies, biographies, blogs, and police reports throughout the years demonstrate a link between such deviant behavior and rock musicians in general, as well as the typical rock listener. Some studies—perhaps not surprisingly—actually show that women who are part of the rock and/or metal culture accept the sexual abuse as commonplace.[8]

Yes, there's evidence that seems to support the caveman metalhead idea. So we should be aware of the kernels of truth associated with metalheads, metal musicians, and metal music. But we shouldn't commit the fallacy of hasty generalization by stereotyping all metalheads.

Cavemen Get a Bad Rap and a Bad Rep

The guys in Sabbath and a lot of other metal musicians may be boneheads when it comes to indulging their animal desires for sex, drugs, and the like. But they're also highly motivated and fairly intelligent. Consider how truly clever, profound, and at times deeply philosophical Geezer Butler's lyrics are in songs like "Wicked World," "Electric Funeral," "After Forever," "Over to You," and basically every song on *Sabbath Bloody Sabbath* and *Sabotage*.

In "War Pigs," for example, Sabbath cleverly and creatively voices the anti-war sentiments of the Vietnam era:

> Generals gathered in their masses / Just like witches at black masses . . . / In the fields the bodies burning / As the war machine keeps turning . . . / Politicians hide themselves away / They only started the war / Why should they go out to fight? / They leave that all to the poor . . . / Treating people just like pawns in chess / Wait 'till their judgment day comes . . .

The last part of the lyrics remind me of that awesome scene from Michael Moore's movie, *Fahrenheit 9/11*, where Moore approached a congressman and asked him if he would consider sending his own son to fight in the Iraq War, and the congressman gave him a look like, "What? Are you F-ing crazy?"

And here's another thing about the claim that metal is made by numskulls for numskulls. That professor I mentioned in the beginning of the chapter, guess what his favorite music was? You guessed right: classical music. As we all know, classical music is usually associated with the most intelligent of our world's lot, so it makes sense that the professor would stick his nose up at metal, right? Now, here's the "this'll-make-you-chuckle," ironic thing about Sabbath and metal in general: Professor John Deathridge (appropriate name, given our subject of metal, isn't it?), King Edward Professor of Music at King's College London, has noted something that a lot of us slightly cultured metalheads have known for some time, namely, "There is a big connection between heavy rock music and Wagner. They (metal musicians) have cribbed quite a lot from 19th Century music."[9] When you listen to parts of Wagner's *Götterdämmerung*, for example, you'd think you were hearing riffs from "Symptom of the Universe," "Megalomania," and "Sabbath Bloody Sabbath." This is because Iommi often used the devil's interval, a tritone (an interval that spans three whole tones). Of course, it was quite appropriate that Sabbath would use the devil's interval, given the close connection between their music and their lyrics, which often dwell on the doom and gloom of evil, destruction, and the Devil.

The classical connection goes beyond the devil's interval, though. Many metal musicians have been trained in classical guitar, piano, and voice, so it makes sense that classical music would make its way into their own specific sound. The guitar work of classically trained Randy Rhoads, Vinnie Moore, Eddie Van Halen, Yngwie

Malmsteen, and Nuno Bettencourt—which, by the way, blows one's mind when one listens to it with an open mind and thinks of the skill involved—has been compared to the violins of a Haydn, Mozart, or Beethoven symphony, and that kind of shredding guitar work is aptly termed Neo-Classical Metal.[10]

Consider, too, the fact that the early Sabbath sometimes sounded similar to progressive rock bands like King Crimson, Emerson, Lake & Palmer, and YES, only heavier. Sabbath, like these progressive bands, constructed songs that were much more complex than the cookie-cutter pop songs of the day that had the standard "introduction, refrain, verse 1, refrain, verse 2, bridge, solo, verse 3, refrain" format. Sabbath's "War Pigs," "Into the Void," "Killing Yourself to Live," and "The Writ" come to mind here. And, it was the complexity that attracted a more enlightened and generally intelligent crowd. So, not only could Sabbath stimulate your senses, but they could stimulate your mind, too.

She Was My Woman . . . I Loved Her So . . .

For all of the shagging Sabbath did, their songs aren't about clubbing women like a caveman. When it comes to women, Sabbath's lyrics differ quite a bit from those of the Rolling Stones, Led Zeppelin, and Kiss. Sabbath's lyrics never boast of sexual conquest or subjugation. Instead, when Ozzy sings to or about a woman, he most often sings of loss, as in "Solitude," "Changes," and "She's Gone" or in appreciation, as in "Sabra Cadabra." Of course, "Dirty Women" from *Technical Ecstasy*, is about prostitutes, but the song doesn't have the feeling of being deeply personal the way the other songs do.[11]

Ozzy and Sharon have had their share of ups and downs, and apparently the two of them can be violent toward one another, but nonetheless they seem to be in a loving relationship. As we know, they have three kids, which can be an indicator (though, not necessarily, of course) of admiration, respect, and love in a relationship. In a 2001 interview with Sharon in *The Guardian*, Ian Gittins wrote: "Her devotion to (Ozzy) is indisputable. 'He's a legend,' (Sharon) says, simply. 'I admire him and I love him.'"[12] And Ozzy has claimed, "I'd be dead. I'd have killed myself by now. Falling in love with Sharon was the best thing that ever happened to me."[13]

Crunchy Pleasure

So the take-home message from this chapter is this: There's evidence for the caveman mentality in metal. But, we shouldn't be too quick to generalize from some to all. Metal music doesn't create cavemen, anyway. At most, it may be the icing on a disordered, dysfunctional, and disillusioned cake. In fact, Rob Halford is wise in noting that alcohol and drug abuse within the contexts of embittered dysfunctional families (usually having father-figures who themselves are cavemen-like) acts as the primary culprit for the genesis of the modern-day caveman; whereas metal music actually provides a relief or escape from the pain.[14] "We give them a great deal of pleasure with our music," Halford claims of the typical teenaged metalhead residing in a dysfunctional family.[15]

Without apologies I relish the incredible way I feel while listening to a track like "Into the Void" with all of its crunchy guitar work, driving rhythms, hypnotic lyrics, and clever melodic turnabouts. So, I say with confidence and non-caveman-like articulation: I am a metalhead. I like Sabbath. I think Sabbath is good music.

Notes

1. Robert Duncan, *The Noise: Notes from a Rock 'n Roll Era* (New York: Ticknor and Fields, 1984), 39.
2. For more on fallacies, see Robert Arp, "The Chewbacca Defense: A *South Park* Logic Lesson," in Robert Arp, ed., *South Park and Philosophy: You Know, I Learned Something Today* (Malden, MA: Wiley-Blackwell, 2006); Jamie Carlin Watson and Robert Arp, *Critical Thinking: An Introduction to Reasoning Well* (London: Continuum Press, 2011).
3. Matt Diehl, "The Holy Sabbath: Ozzy and Tony Talk Drugs, the Devil and How They Invented Heavy Metal," *Rolling Stone*, Issue 948, May 13, 2004.
4. Ibid.
5. Becky Bradway, *Sexual Violence Facts and Statistics* (Springfield, IL: Illinois Coalition Against Sexual Assault, 1993); Alison Lenton and Angela Bryan, "An Affair to Remember: The Role of Sexual Scripts in Perceptions of Sexual Intent," *Personal Relationships* 12 (2005): 483–498; M. Gary Neuman, *The Truth about Cheating: Why Men Stray and What You Can Do to Prevent It* (Malden, MA: Wiley-Blackwell, 2008).

6. Alan Dixson and Matthew Anderson, "Sexual Behavior, Reproductive Physiology and Sperm Competition in Male Mammals," *Physiology & Behavior* 83:2 (2004): 361–371; David Buss, *Evolutionary Psychology: The New Science of the Mind* (Upper Saddle River, NJ: Prentice Hall, 2011).

7. Jeffrey Arnett, "Heavy Metal Music and Reckless Behavior Among Adolescents," *Journal of Youth and Adolescence* 20:6 (1991): 573–592; Jeffrey Jensen Arnett, *Metalheads: Heavy Metal Music And Adolescent Alienation* (Boulder, CO: Westview Press, 1996), 183–188; Keith Kahn-Harris, *Extreme Metal: Music and Culture on the Edge* (New York: Berg Publishers, 2007).

8. Lindsay Timmerman, Mike Allen, Jill Jorgensen, Jennifer Herrett-Skjellum, Michael Kramer, and Daniel Ryan, "A Review and Meta-Analysis Examining the Relationship of Music Content with Sex, Race, Priming, and Attitudes," *Communication Quarterly* 56:3 (2008): 303–324; Felicity Bake and William Bor, "Can Music Preference Indicate Mental Health Status in Young People?" *Australasian Psychiatry* 16:4 (2008): 284–288; Brook Bretthauer, Toni Zimmerman, and James Banning, "A Feminist Analysis of Popular Music: Power Over, Objectification of, and Violence Against Women," *Journal of Feminist Family Therapy* 18:4 (2007): 29–51.

9. Finlo Rohrer, "The Devil's Music," *BBC News Magazine*, Friday, April 28, 2006.

10. Dave Celentano, *Speed Metal: Heavy Metal Neo Classical Styles from Paganini, Bach to Rock* (Anaheim: Centerstream Publications, 2000); William Phillips and Brian Cogan, *Encyclopedia of Heavy Metal Music* (New York: Greenwood Publishing Group, 2009).

11. Thanks to Bill Irwin for these points.

12. Ian Gittins, "'Eminem Sings about Killing His Wife. My Husband Actually Tried to Do It:' Sharon Osbourne Tells Ian Gittins How She Took a Booze-Soaked Rock 'n' Roll Has-Been and Turned Him into a £40 m Industry," *The Guardian*, February 25, 2001.

13. Blabbermouth.net, "Ozzy Osbourne: 'Falling In Love With Sharon was the Best Thing that Ever Happened to Me'," Mirror.co.uk, November 1, 2009.

14. This is Halford's wise claim, but also see the slew of evidence cited in Sherri McCarthy and Caludio Hutz, *Preventing Teen Violence: A Guide for Parents and Professionals* (Westport, CT: Praeger Publishers, 2006).

15. Jon Elliston, "The Subliminal Scares: A Short History of an American Obsession," *Badaboom Gramaphone*, March 3, 2011.

Contributors
Children of the Grave

With big ole headphones on, **Robert Arp** learned to play the drums to *Paranoid*. Many years later, now with Ph.D. in hand and drum sticks on the side, he continues to rock out to Sabbath while teaching and writing philosophy. In addition to scholarly work on the philosophy of mind, Arp is the editor of *South Park and Philosophy*, co-editor of *Batman and Philosophy*, and the co-author of *What's Good on TV? Understanding Ethics through Television*.

James Bondarchuk is just another back street kid who happens to be a Ph.D. student in philosophy at Harvard University. His primary philosophical interests include meta-ethics, epistemology, and the philosophy of Immanuel Kant. Outside of philosophy, he enjoys free food, staying caffeinated, and arguing that *Technical Ecstasy* and *Never Say Die!* are seriously underrated albums. His second favorite band is indeterminate.

Manuel Bremer is professor of philosophy at the University of Düsseldorf, Germany. He works mostly in philosophical logic, philosophy of language, and epistemology. His publications include *An Introduction to Paraconsistent Logics* (2005), *Conceptual Atomism and Justificationist Semantics* (2008), and *Universality in Set Theories* (2010). With current co-author Daniel Cohnitz he wrote *Information* *and Information Flow* (2004). As a dyed-in-the-wool Black Sabbath fan he is not just killing himself to live. His first tattoo was the fallen angel emblem Geezer Butler is said to have designed.

Erich Christiansen is a typical heavy metal guy from a working-class-turned-academic family. He discovered Black Sabbath through his uncle in the seventies, mistakenly thinking "Iron Man" had something to do with the comic book character. Christiansen is working on his Ph.D. in philosophy at the University of Georgia, and is interested in existentialism, Marxism, and the politics and ethics of modern war. He is also a literary writer. He typically warns his students that they may go insane, as he attempts to save their brains.

Daniel Cohnitz is professor of theoretical philosophy at the University of Tartu, Estonia. He is the author of *Information and Information Flow* (with Manuel Bremer), *Nelson Goodman* (with Marcus Rossberg), and a book on thought experiments in philosophy. He has also published a bunch of papers on theoretical philosophy, including the influential philosophy of mind paper "What Is it Like to Eat a Bat?" (with Ozzy Osbourne).

Wesley D. Cray is currently finishing his Ph.D. at the Ohio State University. When he's not turning up the night or making the Devil cry, he can be found hard at work on issues at the intersection of metaphysics and the philosophy of language. Wesley is perhaps most famous for advancing the thesis that, if it seems to be real, it's illusion, and furthermore, that for every moment of truth, there's confusion in life. Look out!

Søren R. Frimodt-Møller holds a Ph.D. in philosophy from the University of Southern Denmark. He is currently affiliated with the Center for Design, Learning and Innovation at Aalborg University's Esbjerg Campus, and is the managing editor of *JMM: The Journal of Music and Meaning*. Frimodt-Møller specializes in formal models for interaction and the role of norms in music performance, and firmly believes that if you *don't* listen to fools, philosophy rules.

Brian Froese is assistant professor of history at Canadian Mennonite University in Winnipeg, Canada. His research interests are centered on the intersection of post-war conservative religion, politics, and culture. Following several religiously haunted strands through the 1950s to the 1980s has led him to consider the use of otherworldly and apocalyptic images in social criticism and reform. In this pursuit, he is pulling together a motley mix of Mennonite pacifists, revival preachers, evangelical pulp writers, horror film directors, and heavy metal artists all exploring the wicked world.

James Heathers is a research scientist and Ph.D. student at the University of Sydney. He is also a professionally angry old man, and sings in Sydney-based death metal band Drillsaw. He writes compulsively, the full catastrophe of which can be seen at www. jamesheathers.com. If you listen to the first five Sabbath albums at the same time while looking profoundly confused, you can hear the sound of inside his head.

Jacob M. Held is associate professor of philosophy at the University of Central Arkansas. He has published on various issues in applied ethics, and political and legal theory in such journals as *Vera Lex, Idealistic Studies, Public Affairs Quarterly*, and *Radical Philosophy Review*. He is also the editor of *James Bond and Philosophy* (with James South) and *Dr. Seuss and Philosophy: Oh, the Thinks You Can Think!* Although he is prone to wearing funny clothes and tinkling bells his classes rarely turn tears into joy, and students aren't always happy when the professor walks by.

William Irwin is professor of philosophy at King's College (Pennsylvania) and Lord of this World of Philosophy and Pop Culture. In addition to publishing in leading philosophy journals, he is the editor of *Metallica and Philosophy, The Matrix and Philosophy, The Simpsons and Philosophy* (with Mark Conard and Aeon Skoble), and *Seinfeld and Philosophy*. The symptom of the universe is written in his eyes.

Dennis Knepp was "introduced to his own mind" at the opening night of Ozzy's 1986 *Ultimate Sin* tour in his hometown of Wichita, Kansas. (Thank you, Dr Ozzy!) He now teaches philosophy at Big Bend Community College in Moses Lake, Washington. His essays can be found in *Twilight and Philosophy, Alice in Wonderland and*

Philosophy, *The Girl with the Dragon Tattoo and Philosophy*, and *The Hobbit and Philosophy*. Don't try to reach Dennis, 'cause he'd tear up your mind; he's seen the future, and he's left it behind.

Greg Littmann is assistant professor of philosophy at Southern Illinois University Edwardsville. He has published in evolutionary epistemology and the philosophy of logic, and has written book chapters for volumes relating philosophy to *The Big Bang Theory*, *Breaking Bad*, *Doctor Who*, *Dune*, *Final Fantasy*, *A Game of Thrones*, Neil Gaiman, *The Onion*, Sherlock Holmes, *The Terminator*, and *The Walking Dead*. Littmann bloody Littmann / Always more to do / 'Cause philosophy is useless / If it never gets to you.

Kevin McCain recently finished a Ph.D. in philosophy at the University of Rochester. He works primarily in the areas of epistemology and philosophy of science. Those are his academic credentials. Now for his Sabbath credentials. Kevin first discovered the joys of Black Sabbath when he was in junior high—and he never forgot them. Throughout high school when others were getting into rap or industrial music his attitude was "if it's not Sabbath (or at the very least Ozzy), why listen to it?" The first concert that Kevin went to as an adult (at the tender age of 18) was the "99" Black Sabbath reunion tour—he describes it in a word, "awesome!" He still thinks that Black Sabbath is clearly the greatest metal band, period. Currently, he is sailing through endless skies where "stars shine like eyes." If you bump into him, it's likely that he'll offer to "give you those things that you thought unreal." After all, he has been known to say that "The sun, the moon, the stars" all bear his seal.

Joel McIver has written 21 books about rock and metal including *Sabbath Bloody Sabbath*, *Justice for All: The Truth about Metallica*, *The Bloody Reign of Slayer*, and *Crazy Train: The High Life and Tragic Death of Randy Rhoads*. He is also a regular contributor to a number of rock and metal magazines. You can often hear him on radio and see him on TV talking about the importance of very loud music. Despite this, he lives a relatively sedate life in the bosom of his family in the leafy county of Buckinghamshire, UK.

Ken Pepper is a Ph.D. student and teaching assistant at the University of York, UK. His research focuses on philosophical problems in cognitive science, and his favorite Sabbath albums are *Master of Reality* and *Heaven and Hell*. Rumor has it that Ken once finished with his woman because she couldn't help him with his philosophy of mind.

Liz Stillwaggon Swan has been enjoying the music and lyrics of Black Sabbath since her high school days and still does, despite her husband's complaint that their music "stinks of the '70s." She credits Black Sabbath with helping to "introduce her to her mind" which has enabled her to earn a Ph.D. in philosophy (University of South Carolina, 2008), become a philosophy teacher, and produce over 20 publications in the areas of cognitive science, philosophy of science, yoga, and music (check out www.lizswan.com for more). The eerie and beautiful masterpiece, "Planet Caravan," is one of her favorite songs ever.

Mark D. White is the chair of the Department of Political Science, Economics, and Philosophy at the College of Staten Island, City University of New York, where he teaches courses that combine economics, philosophy, and law. He is the author of *Kantian Ethics and Economics: Autonomy, Dignity, and Character* (2011) and has edited or co-edited books for the Blackwell Philosophy and Pop Culture series on Batman, *Watchmen*, Iron Man, Green Lantern, the Avengers, and *Downton Abbey*. Although it hasn't worked yet, he still thinks "what is this that stands before me?" is a great pick-up line.

Index

Black Sabbath and Philosophy: Mastering Reality, First Edition. Edited by William Irwin.
© 2013 John Wiley & Sons, Inc. Published 2013 by John Wiley & Sons, Inc.